GOD, GHOSTS, AND THE PARANORMAL MINISTRY

A Supernatural and Spiritual Autobiography

BY REVEREND SHAWN P. WHITTINGTON

Stellium Books

Cover Design by Annette Munnich Stellium Books
All images courtesy of the author
Rev. Shawn Whittington's portraits taken by the talented
Patty Thompson

Featured on our cover: Whittington Castle
The Castle of Wales
Whittington Castle is in northern Shropshire, England, owned and managed by the Whittington Castle Preservation Fund.
Castle St, Whittington, Oswestry SY11 4DF, UK

The site of Whittington Castle dates back to 500 B.C. with the digging of its original trenches. Its current structure stands on 12 acres and was constructed in the 13th Century.

Whittington Castle is open for tours, weddings and other events.

To learn more about, visit, or help support the preservation of Whittington Castle please go to
whittingtoncastle.co.uk

Stellium Books 2019
All Rights Reserved
ISBN: 9781798503898
Manufactured in the USA

And I saw Heaven standing open; and behold, a white horse, and He who sat upon it is called faithful and true, and with justice, He judges and wages war. And his eyes are like a flame of fire, and on his Head are diadems... And he is clothed in a garment sprinkled with blood, and His name is called the word of God, and the armies of Heaven, clothed in fine linen, white and pure, were following Him on white horses... And He has on his garment and on His thigh a name written, "King of Kings, and Lord of Lords"

Revelation

Dedication

I would like to dedicate, thank, and acknowledge, my parents, Lawrence William Whittington, (September 1918 – February 2011) and Edith Morace Whittington, (September 1925 – February, 2012.) Thank you both for taking time out of your busy schedules as angels, to help me write this book from the other side. May you rest in peace...

To my sisters, Pam and Paula, and my brother, Spencer. Other more wonderful siblings do not exist on this earth. To this, and many more lifetimes as a family to come. Love, Shawn

To my much better half - my wife, Sharon Whittington, for without whom I would have never had the courage or push to have written this book. All my love, in our past life, this one, and the next. I love you, Shawn

And finally, to all my mentors and colleagues that got me here (you know who you are).

"May you be buried in a coffin, made of a thousand-year-old oak tree, that I'm going to plant for you tomorrow!" Irish Blessing

God, Ghosts, and the Paranormal Ministry: A Supernatural, and Spiritual Autobiography by The Reverend Shawn Patrick Whittington (Ordained Exorcism-Deliverance Minister Advanced Practice.)

Through Divine intervention, Reverend Shawn was created by God to be on his current path and to be doing exactly what he is doing today. And, that is simply to push back the darkness that is closing in on the world around us.

Born of a long ancestry of warriors for Christ, the Whittingtons of England (on his Father's side), and a long lineage of devoutly religious, and spiritual people, The Moraces of Brazil (on his Mother's side), a.k.a. "The Rev" has spent a lifetime as a ghostbuster, paranormal investigator, and today, an exorcist.

A book unlike anything you've read yet, or ever will read. A book that's longer than a lifetime in the making, and for the reader, a journey through realms of the supernatural that for many, until now, have just been stories. Please take extreme precautions when reading a book the devil doesn't want you to read.

God Bless,
Rev. Shawn Whittington

Introduction

"That thing upstairs is not my son, what have they done with my baby?" These words and this question were spoken to me by an almost hysterical Mother while standing in her front yard wearing only her house robe. She was too frightened to be inside her own home. I quickly realized I was going to have to go inside this home and face whatever it was inside, ALL alone. This was the very first case that came across my desk after becoming an ordained deliverance minister. God put me right to work! This was the case that changed my life and made me realize beyond a shadow of a doubt, that I was indeed, truly created before I was born, to do this deliverance ministry.

I will finish telling the story of this incredible case later in the book. I also feel I must explain exactly what I mean by created before I was born to do this. In order to do this, I must go back to the beginning. When I say beginning, I really mean the beginning. I would like to take you back to 1077, Whittington, England, and just know that this story goes even further back...

Table of Contents

1. Warriors for Christ	1
2. Catholicism and Spirituality	9
3. A Calling	17
4. Never Too Young	25
5. All Grown Up	33
6. Vegas Supernatural	45
7. Home Is Where The Heart Is	55
8. They Run In A Pack	67
9. Man With No Face	83
10. The Holy Spirit	97
11. Black Dogs And Beasts	107
12. Paranormal Ministry	125
13. The Final Chapter Part I and Part II – (Exorcism by Distance)	151
14. Prayers	185
15. Photo Gallery	191

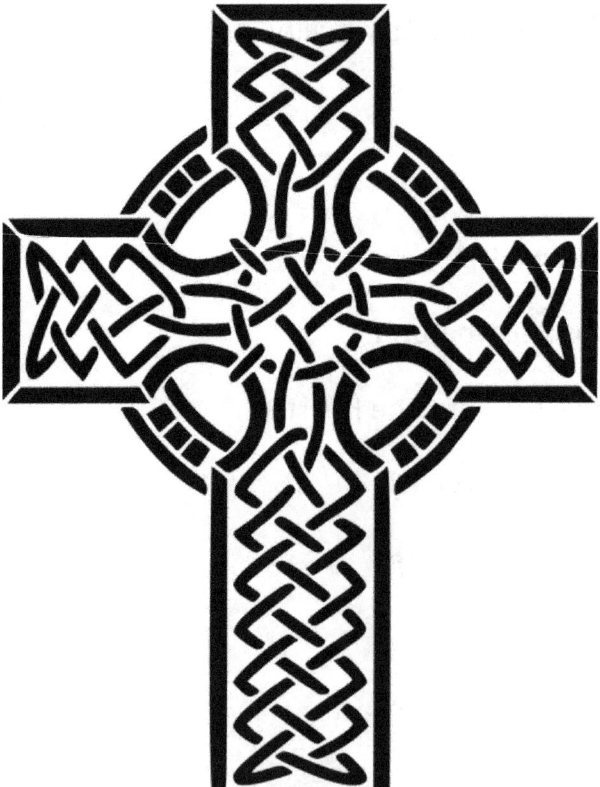

1
Warriors for Christ

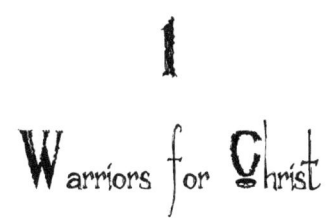

Inheritance. It comes in many forms. My inheritance is my blood. Great heritage on both sides of the family. My Father's side, the Whittingtons from England and my Mother's side, the Moraces, from Brazil.

The Whittingtons, my Father's ancestry, is that of a long lineage of warriors for Christ. The story handed down through the generations has been of mystery, and the supernatural, with one underlying common thread, good versus evil. In ancient times, the area which is now Whittington, England, had a couple of different names. We know one was Whitton or Witon. The other was Whitetown. Eventually, it was founded by Whittingtons and became Whittington, England.

The Whittingtons had ties to the church, and many of them were priests. They built the Church of Whittington and the parish of Whittington. At some point in time, a religious sect similar to the Knights Templar, not that sect, but another order arrived in Whittington, and it is believed this order was in possession of the Holy Grail. The Grail was given to the Whittingtons for safe keeping. It is said that the Grail was then buried beneath one of the churches in Whittington. Sometime later, when the search for the Grail went through a heated period, the fear that it might fall into wrong hands, a priest with the last name of Whittington is said to have been given the formidable task of getting the Grail out of England. This priest did just that, accomplishing to get the Grail all the way to America, and today it is thought to be buried somewhere in Maryland.

Whittingtons flourished and thrived all up and down the East coast. My Father's immediate blood relatives migrated Westward and settled in Oklahoma. When they first arrived in that part of the country, what later became Oklahoma was referred to as Indian Territory at that time.

Those Whittingtons, my Father's great grandparents, grandparents, Mother, and Father were very Quaker-like in the sense they worked with the indigenous people of the area, bringing the English language, and their religious belief system to the natives. It goes without saying, there was a fair amount of integrating between the Whittingtons, and the Native Americans. There is some Native American blood flowing through my veins too. Throughout this book, I will from time to time travel back in time to discuss certain aspects of my ancestry that directly tie into many things that I have seen, and experienced throughout my many years as a ghostbuster, and now an ordained registered exorcism deliverance minister. I know that I was created to do exactly what I am doing today, and where I am at in life now, was pre-determined long before I was born. I will start with my Father and his guardian angel. I hope to meet my Father's guardian angel one day, I have a great big thank-you to give to either him or her.

My Father was born and raised in Wyandotte, Oklahoma. He was a great athlete. He played on a high school football team that was comprised of almost all Native American young men. My Father remains on a list of one of the 100 best high school athletes to ever come out of Oklahoma. Guess who else is on that list? Jim Thorpe.

My Father lived through the great depression, and many times he and I would sit together, and he would reminisce about his adventures hopping freight trains from town to town to find work. He did this with his very best buddy from childhood, a man named, Troy.

According to my Dad, Troy was the best bare-fisted boxer – fighter he ever saw, which was another way they made money riding the rails.

Eventually, Troy enlisted in the Army, and my Father enlisted in the Navy. Many years passed by without them seeing one another until their paths crossed again just before the great war. Troy had suffered a severe injury in a grenade accident almost blowing both his legs off.

He was confined to a hospital bed in the Philippines. My Father visited Troy there, and that was the last time they would see each other in this world. My Father had a choice to make, stay with Troy until he passed, and then join the Philippine Guerillas, or get aboard one of the last Navy ships leaving the island before the Japanese arrived. Troy actually was the one who convinced my Dad to leave. As my Father walked out of that hospital room, Troy said to him, "Stub, I sure wish we could just hop a train, and get the hell out of here!"

I always feel a lot of emotion telling this story, because I remember how emotional my Dad would get every time he told it to me. My Dad said he saw Troy's spirit from time to time years later, and Troy always looked young, strong, and walking on two legs. Even more amazing was many years later in my life while watching one of my favorite paranormal reality show (a real one), the team investigated an old abandoned bombed out military hospital in the Philippines. They contacted the spirits of many fallen heroes. This just happened to be the same hospital Troy died in. That episode was also very emotional for me.

The time, the beginning of World War II. My Father, Lawrence William Whittington, was a twenty plus year retired Chief Radioman from The U.S. Navy. He fought in World War II, Korea, was a Purple Heart recipient and finished his naval career in Naval Intelligence.

He had already been enlisted in the Navy for a short period of time prior to the bombing of Pearl Harbor. When Pearl Harbor was attacked by the Japanese, the powers that be knew the Japanese would next invade the Philippines.

My Father was stationed aboard the USS Pecos, which was docked in Subic Bay, Philippines. All Naval personnel were ordered to evacuate the Island, and all naval vessels ordered to get underway. Shortly after getting underway, and making it out to open ocean, the USS Pecos engaged the enemy, came under attack and was sunk. My Father stayed aboard the ship until the last possible moment, sending out their situation, and location on the teletype, morse code, and radio. He got out of the radio shack moments before a kamikaze plane crashed into the top of the ship destroying the whole communications section of the ship.

Moments before my Father had sent a young sailor back into the radio shack to retrieve some supplies when the plane struck, killing the young sailor. My Father never forgave himself for that, and many years later before my Father passed, He told me the ghost of that sailor visited him a few times to let him know he was ok, and always had a smile on his face.

My Father went into the water at mid-day, and hanging onto a piece of gangplank, floated in the water until the morning of the following day. He bobbed up and down in the water, which had God knows what floating on top, oil, gasoline, etc., and remembers how terrifying it was not to know if help was coming and to listen to the cries of dying and drowning men off in the darkness.

Little did anyone know that no help was coming. All Naval vessels in the area were ordered not to go back for survivors because the area was too hot with the enemy. The only reason anyone else knew of the sinking of the USS Pecos was because my Father stayed until the end to make sure the message and call for help went out. Another one of the true heroes of the story was the captain of the ship that did go back. This captain ignored orders and turned his ship around.

By morning, my Father was very weak and very ill from having swallowed mouthfuls of ocean water throughout the night accidentally while bobbing up and down. When the sun came up over the horizon, there was a thick fog and mist over the water. My Father even wondered if he had already died, because the fog was so thick and it was deadly silent.

Then off in the distance, he could hear the engines of an approaching ship. He knew he wasn't dead, but considered he might be soon for he was certain that was an enemy vessel, as the ship was almost upon him. The fog lifted, and to his extreme astonishment, it was a U.S. Navy ship. The ship stopped, turned off its engines and began throwing life preservers, ropes, and any other floating items over the side, including rope ladders. He knew he would have to kick hard to make it to the ship. He couldn't let go of the gangplank and swim because he was just too weak. Some time passed, and he was almost to the ship when he heard a voice over a loudspeaker say, "Attention, there has been enemy ships reported in the area, prepare to get underway."

He then heard the ship's engines turn over. He knew he couldn't make it, and saw a rope floating in the water next to him. He thought to himself, they are going to drag me back dead, but they are not leaving me here.

He began to wrap the rope in between his legs, around his waist, chest, and shoulders. He actually felt the slack of the rope tighten and the feeling of being pulled as the ship began to move. He then heard a deep voice say, "There's one more in the water." He looked up, and saw a very large muscular sailor jump over the side, and while hanging on to the ship with one hand, reached down with the other hand and grabbed my Father by the scruff of the neck, lifted him out of the water, and tossed him onto the deck of the ship. My Father remembers hitting the deck, then waking up with medical personnel working on him, and he was under a tent, on the very same spot he had landed. He was told he had been there unconscious for two days. When he was finally well enough to get to his feet, he conducted a thorough investigation aboard the ship to find this sailor who saved his life. He could not find one sailor who fit the description, nor any sailor who knew of another sailor that fit that description. The most amazing thing is that no one could even remember having witnessed the incident. Some said it was like one moment my Father wasn't there, then in the next moment, he was. My Father all his life truly believed his guardian angel saved him that day. My Mother, my Sisters, my Little Brother, and I know that's what happened. This was an extremely credible man who obtained the highest top secret status available in the Navy at the time and finished his Naval career working on the staff for the Ambassador to Brazil. This man was truth.

2
Catholicism and Spirituality

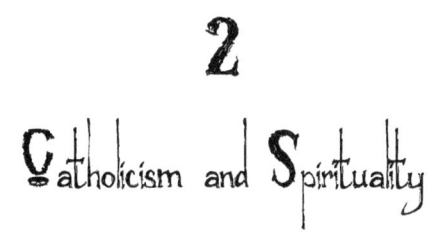

Well, it's Saturday, September 2nd, 2017, and I'm off and running, and writing this book. Today is my 15th wedding anniversary. By the time I get through with this book, you will have gotten to know my better half and the other member of Ghost-B-Gone.biz (the ministry). She came to me today and asked me to finally stop with all the excuses and start writing. She said before you're too old, I'm already old, and before God forbid something happens and you can't write it, as an anniversary gift to me, please write your book. I listen for a living, so I'm listening now, and for what it's worth here goes. There is no telling how long of a journey this will be. I find myself having to dig deep at times to uncover things in my past that dredge up so much emotion. Emotions I try to avoid because I have been known to be a bit of a cry baby from time to time.

I'm also a real "Momma's boy." So, speaking of Momma's Boy, it's time I introduced you to my Mother, Edith Morace Whittington, born and raised in

Cruz Dasalmas, Brazil, a little town in the North of Bahia, up in the mountains. Cruz Dasalmas means Soul's Cross. This little gem of a town was once on the Guinness Book of World Records as the town with the most churches in it. This is a very spiritual place. I have not yet been there, but friends, cousins, and family members who have been there say there is no veil between the living and the dead there. The dead walk around as though they are still living their lives among the living. It is a common and natural occurrence there. I have childhood photos of my older sisters when they were growing up there, where you can clearly see spirits in the photos with them. My Mother was baptized Catholic, and very devout in her worship of Christ. She was also very spiritual.

She once told me when I was ten that I would see a lot of ghosts in my life, and not to be afraid, that ghosts were just people that didn't have a body anymore. She said if one shows itself to you there is a reason, and for me to ask them what it is they want. Simple right?!

My Mother met, fell in love with, and married my Father in Brazil after the Great War while he was stationed in Brazil. My two older sisters were both born there. After a few years of marriage, while my sisters were very young, they moved back to the

United States, because my Father got orders re-assigning him to a Naval base in Northern California. My Mother didn't know at that time that she could never return to Brazil. My Mother left behind her whole life, and the coffee plantation she grew up on.

After living on the Naval base in California for a while, my Father went out to sea on one of his many Naval adventures. Months had passed, and it was now time for my Father's ship to return. My Mother was extremely happy, she missed my Father terribly, and it was difficult raising my two older sisters on her own, in a country she could barely speak the language. My Father's ship arrived, and the phone rings. My Mother answers, and it is the base Doctor calling from the base hospital. Somehow, while gone on his cruise, he contracted Spinal Meningitis, Cephalitis, and a few other complications, and was dying. My Father apparently was out of his mind, trying to hurt people, and himself. They had him strapped to a hospital bed, and he had slipped into a coma. The Doctor told my Mother that they didn't expect my Father to live until morning, and if she wanted to see him again, she needed to come to the hospital at once.

Absolutely out of her mind, my Mother arranged for a neighbor to come watch my sisters. She calls a cab and heads out to the hospital. On the way to the hospital, my Mother stops at the base church. She goes inside and prays to St. Jude to petition on her behalf for God to save my Father's life.

In return for this, my Mother promised from that day on, whenever she went to church, she would do it crawling on her hands and knees. She also promised to have another child. The birth of my second oldest sister was very difficult on my Mother, and it was recommended to her by many Doctors that she should not have any more children. So, the petition and promises were made, and she headed on toward the hospital. At the hospital, it was just as she was warned about, he was in a coma, strapped down to his bed, and appeared to be living out his last moments on earth. She sat at his bedside, held his hand, prayed, prayed, and kept on praying until she fell asleep.

She woke up to the most amazing sight she had ever seen, my Father was sitting up in bed looking at her, and asked her, "Edith, what am I doing in the hospital, and what am I doing tied down to the bed?!" She jumped up, screamed for the nurses and doctors, and stood staring at my Father in amazement. The hospital staff too was amazed. Every test imaginable was run on my Father, and no trace of the disease could be found. My Mother kept her promise to God.

From that day on, whenever she went to mass, she did it crawling on her hands and knees, until she got too old and physically unable to do so. She also had another child, TA-DAH, ME, yours truly! She always referred to me as her miracle baby, I never argued that with her, and allowed her to call me that her whole life. She also went on to also have my little brother who is a great guy also. I love him and I'm very proud of him too. So, that's my family, my Father, Mother, two older sisters, and a younger brother. My oldest sister is a school teacher, my younger brother is a special needs school teacher, and my 2nd oldest sister is a great Mother too, one of the most devout Catholics and spiritually connected persons I know, and works at the happiest place on earth, Disneyland! See, I told you I had a great family. My Mother baptized and confirmed me in the Catholic faith under St. Patrick as my guardian saint, along with my guardian angel, who looks like a young Susan Sarandon, and of course St. Jude too.

    Something I take from my Mother that I use in my approach to demonic cases as an exorcist is, I always drop to my knees at the front door of a demonically infested location, say a prayer to St. Jude, and crawl on my hands and knees over the threshold into the home. DEMONS HATE THAT!! Thank-you Mom.

Something my Mother always regretted was that she never made it back to Brazil before she died. I am happy to announce though that a beautiful woman came to visit me one night, then walked right through my door and into my living room. I followed her only to find my Mother sitting there crying tears of joy. At that moment the phone rang. It was my Mom's sister calling from Florida to let my Mom know that their Mother had just passed away in Brazil. So, at least she got to see her Mother before she went to heaven. That always gave my Mom a lot of closure. I miss you, Mom...

I recently had two psychics that I'm good friends with, two of the few I can count on one hand that I truly feel walking the Christ light, reach out to me with messages from both my Dad and my Mom. Among the messages, two were the same, my Mom and Dad both said they would help me write this book. Every time I grab a pen and put it to paper, I can feel them guiding it, and can feel and hear their thoughts. Your loved ones never leave you.

So my family, my oldest sister, Pam, is a school teacher and growing up it was always like she was my second Mother. The secrets we have shared and the things she knows about me that no one else knows, good, bad, embarrassing, you name it could be another novel! Pam also inherited being a great Mom herself from our Mother for sure. She is a devout Catholic, very spiritual and sensitive in her own way. She continues to receive messages from the other side meant for me to this day. She always seems to show up at the right time when I really need to hear a message through her. My second oldest sister, Paula, the Brazilian bloodline runs thick in her. She has the long dark hair, dark skin, not black but darker than me, and I think she would be perfectly fine with living in Brazil. Paula is "the talent" in the family! She is a wonderfully blessed artist, drawing and painting. She has sold many of them, and many are on display in galleries. She, I feel is the most spiritual of my immediate family. A devout Catholic, but is absolutely no stranger to spirit. Paula has a passion for, and also an extreme respect for the paranormal. She has over the years given me a lot of advice on many things regarding the other side. Paula could have been anything she wanted to be, and because she and Pam are so much like our Mother she too became a great and loving Mother herself.

Spencer, my younger brother is just a really good guy, everyone loves him, and I regret not being a better big brother to him. He and I are very much alike, and unlike one another if that makes any sense. He has all the personal characteristics I wish I had. He is very smart. I'm a high school dropout, he's a college graduate. He is Catholic and has a healthy respect also for the paranormal, but I guess because his sisters and brother are so over the top with it, he perhaps feels someone in this family should represent some sense of normalcy. He is also a special needs school teacher. See, I told you he is smart, and compassionate too. I don't think there is anyone other than my Father and Mother when they were alive even now, that I can always count on more, and that is Spencer... So, not sure if Pam, Paula, and Spencer will read this, but if they do, I want them to know if we all get another shot at this in our next lives, I'll be a better brother.

3
A Calling

What I did not want this book to be is someone's ancestry research journal or just a prayer book. I did feel it necessary to include some of my family history, and include a few of the strongest prayers one can use to combat evil. There will be some case studies only to demonstrate how true evil can manifest, and how things can go terribly wrong when one enters into spiritual warfare unprepared. I want this book to help people avoid being put into a situation in which an unholy spirit feels it has been invited and has permission to attach itself to someone. AND, God forbid, if that happens, to be able to draw a line in the sand, fight back, and know where to go to get help. Ultimately though, if you are the target through your fault or not, only you with the help of the Holy Spirit can command these malevolent entities in the name of Jesus Christ to go to the foot of the cross for Jesus to deal with. But, you must have FAITH!

If you don't have faith now, or any religious belief system in place, perhaps you will after you have finished this book, and if not at least keep this book handy to be able to put into the hands of someone you love who might need it. It's all intent brothers and sisters. Pray to whatever higher power you want to as long as it's one of love, and light. Your strongest weapons against evil are humility and love. Hate the sin, love the sinner. If you're an atheist, I'm so sorry, but you have not been more wrong about anything in your whole life! I hope this book changes your outlook, because I assure you, the Holy Trinity is real! God the Father, God the Son, and the Holy Spirit are very real!!

If you are pagan, wiccan, satanist, devil worshiper, or witch, I pray for you too, because the devil is very real too, and I'm going to miss all of you in heaven. Where you're headed is someplace completely different. Well, that's as preachy as I'm going to get, I'm not that kind of reverend...

It should come as no surprise to you that I know I was created to be exactly where I'm at doing now. Having said that I'm still amazed at how far I have come on this journey since I was a young boy. Only young boys get "the talk" from their Fathers, and I did get that talk from my Father when I was a young boy, but I also got "the talk" from my Mother too when I was around ten years old. This speech was very different than what most Mother's give to their child. It went something like this – she confirmed that I would do something great for God one day. She also told me that I would see a lot of ghosts in my life, and not to be afraid of them, that they were just people that didn't have a body anymore, that if a spirit showed itself to me it meant they wanted something from me or needed to give me a message. Ask the spirit what they want, and how you can help. If they give you a message fine, if they ask for help, try to help. If you can't, be honest and tell them you can't, and to please not bother you anymore. How she knew that I would see a lot of ghosts in my life I don't know, but man o' man was she right....

I remember being a bit freaked out, and when I did see spirit I would try my best to ignore them. For some strange reason, and it's the same even today, spirits would mostly come to me while I slept. The dreams would be so vivid, they would wake me right up. The spirits would also get a little touchy-feely and grab me while I slept, which would launch me out of a dead sleep.

I would take naps with my Mother when I was young, and she would tell me to hold onto her hair while she held my leg to prevent anything from taking me while we slept. That freaked me out too.

Sometimes I would wake up, and see someone I didn't know looking down at me, and I would just hold onto my Mother's hair tighter, and close my eyes. When I opened my eyes, there's my Mother praying, and putting a necklace on me, and telling me to go back to sleep. I would come to find out later, that it was actually a crucifix, St. Christopher, St. Patrick, or St. Michael medal she would put around my neck. Yes, I was baptized Catholic. I was both baptized, and later confirmed under St. Patrick as my guardian saint. So you can imagine St. Patrick's Day was always a big deal. Mom always made sure I had something green to wear and made sure I came home to as authentic an Irish dinner as possible and did OK considering she was Brazilian.

Later on, the something green to wear and authentic Irish dinners were replaced by the family kilt and shots of single malt Irish whiskey, and pints of dark Irish lager/stout. Those were the days, and thank God I don't drink anymore. I might as well get this out of the way, for many years I was a raging alcoholic. Every stupid thing I ever did, and every bad thing that ever happened to me, happened when I was drunk. You absolutely, positively cannot be an active practicing alcoholic and engage in battle with the beast.

While we're at it, might as throw illegal drugs in there too. My lowest points consisted of using marijuana, cocaine, crack, meth, and acid just to name a few. I made mention of it earlier, these unholy entities look for any open door to walk through, and move right in. They look at it as though you accepted their invitation, and temptation to accept these things, substances, what have you, and therefore invited them to attach to you. Once this attachment has taken place, you are then brought to the attention of the one they serve, the devil. Quickly, for those of you not quite sure who the devil is, the devil is a psychopathic murderer who sat on the throne next to his creator, God, and then tried to murder him and take over Heaven. In this book, I will introduce you to this, the one they call, the liar, the dragon, the evil one, the lord of the flies, among other things, and the legion of disgusting creatures that do his bidding.

Long before I became the ordained exorcism deliverance minister I am today, I'm going to take you back to that ten-year-old boy who was just starting his ghost-busting journey. Cases I felt I failed at, and some I'm proud of and brought closure to. Later the journey will get quite dark.

You will have to put on your big boy and big girl pants, grab your Holy Water, Bible, Crucifix, and I will take you through eight demonic cases my wife, Sharon, and I worked in a row. During those cases, Sharon and I both became survivors of extreme demonic attacks, resulting in Sharon battling three rare forms of cancer, and my attack being severe enough for me to leave this ministry, for good I thought until something had other plans for me. I will also include some very powerful deliverance prayers I do not leave home without, and my most recent and most effective technique for cleansing and blessing property, homes, and individuals. Most of all I pray, whether you have been called to this ministry or simply intrigued by my story, take precautions when reading this book.

***

Prayer of Command

In His name, and by the power of His cross and blood, I ask Jesus to bind any evil spirits, forces, and powers of the earth, air, fire, or water, of the netherworld, and the satanic forces of nature. By the power of the Holy Spirit, and by His authority, I ask Jesus Christ to break any curses, hexes, or spells, and send them back to where they came from, if it be His Holy will. I beseech Thee Lord Jesus to protect us by pouring Thy precious blood on us, (my family, friends, and all in this ministry work) which Thou hast shed for us, and I ask thee to command that any departing spirits leave quietly, without disturbance, and go straight to Thy Holy Cross to dispose of as Thou sees fit. I ask Thee to bind any demonic interaction, interplay or communications. I place (this book and its readers), under the protection of the blood of Jesus Christ which he shed for us. **Amen.**

4
Never Too Young

So, fresh off my Mother's talk with me about ghosts, I'm ready, or so I thought. I was a very active kid, and had lots of friends, and lived a double life, kind of. When the urge hit me to go do something scary, I would go exploring. I grew up in the San Fernando Valley in Southern California. You could go riding your bike deep into Topanga Malibu Canyons, go hiking and explore all the old abandoned movie sets, wood shacks, Indian grounds, etc. It was all innocent, you didn't even have any equipment. Well, unless you count a canteen, knife, magnifying glass and compass. When the time came to consider stepping up my game because I saw some old ghost investigator guy on the news with a bunch of stuff, I had no clue as to what it was, I started carrying an old Polaroid camera. The one with the flash bar you would mount on top and the film would pop and develop in your hand. Later, I graduated to the polaroid with the built-in flash. I was usually by myself and got spooked all the time. I wasn't the most successful ghost hunter.

Looking back on things, I'm not sure what I thought I would find, and capture on camera, or why I was even trying, because I saw spirit all the time. I realize now that many of the spirits I saw were probably ancestors. Especially if the apparition was native American or very European looking, from the UK to be more exact. Our ancestors act as protectors and guides even though I understand that we also have actual guides that act something different.

I'm a big believer in Guardian Angels and I have seen mine twice. At least I think it's my Guardian Angel. I have also been told your Guardian Angels are also spirit guides and loved ones who have crossed over. My Guardian Angel, spirit guide, ancestor, whomever or whatever she is, look exactly like Susan Sarandon. A young Susan Sarandon from the original Rocky Horror Picture Show time in her career. She also saved my life twice, and I also owe her a big thank-you when we meet one day. The first time we met I was swimming at the beach and got caught in a rip tide. I ended up trying to climb up on a big rock protruding out of the water. It was covered with barnacles, and every time I would just get out of the water, and end up on the rock, a wave would come and knock me off back into the sea.

This happened several times, and I got so exhausted. I was dog paddling, and barely able to keep my head above water. I was too far offshore and knew I didn't have the strength to make the swim to shore. I started to go under and really thought this could be it. All of a sudden this girl is in the water floating right next to me. All she had above water was her head. She smiled at me, and said, "Take my hand, and swim this way."

I said, "I can't, I'm too tired." Her hand came up out of the water, and she smiled. I grabbed her hand, and an overwhelming sense of calm came over me.

We swam together sideways to the shoreline about 50 yards. She then turned toward land, and continued to swim with me, until she looked at me, and said, "Put your feet down, and walk the rest of the way in."

I realized I could touch bottom, and I was now only chest deep in the water. I stumbled onto the land and fell face first in the sand totally spent. A few seconds later, a lifeguard walked up, and asked me if I was ok?! I said, "I am now, this girl here helped me."

He said, "What girl?" I looked up, looked out into the water, looked left and right, and she was gone! I thought of her often, and it would be many years later, she would come into my life again.

We all go through challenging times in our lives. Whether you are aware of it or not, our lives are a roller coaster ride through the world of spiritual warfare. And, those of us called to this ministry are even that much more of a target. I know now, that every dark time in my life, I was under attack. My Guardian Angel stepped in again in my twenties to save my life.

I drank way too much at a going away party for a friend and stayed way too late, and then tried to make a long drive home. One moment I'm driving on the freeway, and the next moment I'm abruptly woken up by a girl sitting next to me in the front seat of my truck yelling, "Turn, turn!"

I looked up, and see that its Susan Sarandon again, I look forward and I'm driving straight for a cliff. I crank the steering wheel sharply to the left, and my truck fishtails just avoiding going over the edge, and now I'm flying back across all the freeway lanes, and smash head-on into the concrete center divider, and wake up days later in a hospital bed with just a broken arm. While in the hospital, the ambulance driver came to visit me and told me that while I was unconscious, I was holding a conversation with someone about my life, and decisions. He said I came to once, and asked him if the girl I was with in my truck was OK. He told me there was no girl, and I smiled and dozed back off. After leaving the hospital, I went to see my truck. The roof was smashed down onto the front seats, and the engine pushed back into the cab, and up against the seats. Somehow my body fell into a tiny little space that allowed me to survive.

Divine intervention my friends. You will hear about that happening again in this book. I want you all to know it happens, and guardian angels do exist, and that is why I pray to mine every day. And you should too!

I was cited for DUI for this incident, and the sad thing is, I still continued to drink. It wasn't until many, many years later after my wife, and I both survived extreme demonic attacks that I finally quit drinking. I have been sober for a long time, and ask that you pray for me to remain sober.

I'm not going to lie, I had a little bit of Dennis the Menace in me when I was young. I learned at a young age, just when you think you have it all under control with spirit, spirit and reality will throw a monkey wrench into the works. My first up close and personal face to face physical, and psychic encounter happened at a home my sisters were renting with some friends, not too far from where I was living with my parents.

The movie, The Burbs, always reminds me of this house. Newer neighborhood, with that one old out of place home that doesn't seem to belong, and the rent is cheap. Guess why? Haunted! I went there to go spend the night and was not told about the ghost until I had already been there a while, and it was bedtime. I know, right! I'm in a sleeping bag on the floor of the living room next to the fireplace. All I can hear is the snap, crackle, and pop of the burning fire. The fire is my only light too.

One of several friends of my sisters spending the night came walking downstairs. When she made it to the bottom floor, she began to dance slowly across the floor. Danced right up to my sleeping bag, and looked at me, smiled and held her hand out to me. When my fingers touched hers, you know when you shuffle across the carpet with your socks on, touch someone and give them a shock, that's exactly what happened to me, but much more intense. Her touch was also ice cold. I suddenly realized I could see my breath, and then she is speaking to me, but her lips were not moving. She told me her story, and I'll keep that between her and I. She continued to dance right into the fireplace and vanished. I quickly jumped out of the sleeping bag, ran upstairs, and jumped in bed with my sisters.

By dawns early light, things didn't seem so scary, and I started entertaining thoughts that I might just really be cut out for this ghost investigating thing. Couldn't get any worse than that right? Wrong!

Shortly after that, the whole family went to see the premiere of the Exorcist. Long story short, came home from that movie, threw my Ouija board out, and any black light posters I had that seemed in the least bit dark and creepy, made it to the trash too. Then I slept with my parents for a week. Honestly, I'm still a big believer that kids shouldn't be allowed to get involved in the paranormal until they're a little older. I was 14.

5
All Grown Up

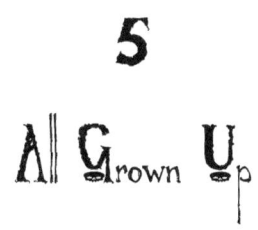

I've had a good life. I'm fifty-eight now, and I figure if I'm lucky, I have maybe thirty years left. One can do a lot of good things for others in that amount of time remaining. I have been blessed more than one man deserves in a lifetime. I'm sure I have made some people upset with me here and there, that's life. I would be very surprised, but more so very hurt if I found out I had any real enemies. I do not hold that degree of anger toward anyone. I was a good athlete when I was young. It didn't matter the sport, but I excelled in football. I got that talent from my Father. To this day my Father remains on an official list as one of the one hundred best high school athletes ever to come out of Oklahoma.

His sport was football too! I played many years of organized youth football. During these years of school, friends, and trying to just be a regular kid, I continued to read the occasional book on ghosts, explore abandoned buildings, and homes when I came across them, and those very close to me knew they could confide in me if they were having paranormal issues, and I would try to help.

I broke my leg playing football and was never the same. As my desire to play dwindled, so did my desire to stay in school, and I dropped out of high school to pursue another passion, dancing! Don't laugh!!

That's right, dancing. I became a street dancer. My style was called Locking. My street dancing nickname was "Panda." I am proud of the fact though, that for about a ten year stretch there from the early '80s to the early '90s, I was considered by my peers to be the funkiest, and best Locker in the world! I managed to appear in several videos, a couple of T.V. shows, a movie and a lot of touring.

I know, you're wondering what all this had to do with the paranormal. I used to frequent an underground dance club called, "Radio". Radio was located in the basement of an old, rundown, abandoned apartment building in one of the oldest, and roughest areas of old downtown Los Angeles.

This underground club was run by some of the most hardcore street gangsters, and hoodlums in that area. All the best street dancers were allowed (by invitation only), to attend this happening, many upcoming guest Rappers and D.J.'s like Ice T, and Un Glove would also perform there.

    Many talent scouts and agents also attended these dances looking for the best dancer to hire for television and film. I got a lot of work by hanging out at Radio. One night after battling for hours, I decided to take a walk around the block, get some fresh air, and wind down before a long drive home. I noticed a hospital across the street, and a nurse standing at the bottom of the walkway leading to the emergency entrance.

    She was staring at me with a smile on her face, so I decided to cross the street and say, "Hi." We had a nice, but brief one-sided conversation.

    She asked me if I was okay, and if I was staying out of trouble?! She said, "I have to get back now."She turned around, and headed back up the walk, entered the hospital through one side of a double door leading to Emergency. Don't know why, but I walked up to the doors, looked through the windows of the doors, and it was pitch black in the hospital. Wait a minute, I thought, I tried the handles on the doors, and they were locked. I took a few steps back, looked up at the building, and noticed not one window had any light coming through it. Didn't give it much thought other than, man you're tired, and alone in a bad part of town, you need to get your butt home. Which is exactly what I did.

Many years later, I found out the hospital was Linda Vista. It had been closed for a number of years before the night of my experience, and it just so happens , that Linda Vista is one of the most haunted locations in the world!

See, that's what my dancing and the paranormal had to do with one another. The world of the supernatural is around all the time, and if you're lucky (or not) you might just find yourself standing in an opening in the veil. I'm not done yet!

One special night stands out to me, more so than most. It's the night the dance crew I was with at the time, got hired to perform at the wrap party for Ghostbusters 2! Yeah, I know!! I knew the performance would do well, I was more concerned with getting to meet Bill or Dan?! The party took place under a huge (I mean huge) tent like a circus big top in the middle of an open lot in Westwood, California.

The performance did go well, and afterward, while mingling, I found myself standing next to the one and only, Bill Murray! He actually complimented me on the group's dance performance. All I wanted to do was talk about ghostbusting with him, and he wanted to talk about learning how to breakdance. We did have a nice personal conversation about his wanting to break away from the comedic roles, and do more serious acting.

He was excited to be getting ready to film "Razors Edge". I saw it, liked it, and thought Bill was good in it. But, Mr. Murray, you were blessed, and I mean blessed with the gift to make people laugh. So, it is what it is. He did wish me the best in my dancing, and acting career if I made that switch, and also added, if I chose to continue to pursue my passion at ghostbusting, a more honorable profession I won't find?! As he walked away I said, "Bill," he looked back and I said, "and you Sir will forever be for me, when someone asks who 'ya gonna call?"I didn't say another word and just pointed at him.

He smiled, turned, and walked over to the bar, ordered a drink, and began to bullshit with Sean Penn, and Robert Duvall. Well, as time and the years went on, this lifestyle opened up doors that I was unaware of, and one day I realized that I was a drug addict. Never did heroin, but tried and used just about everything else on the menu frequently.

I also know that there were very dark forces at work here keeping me in this lifestyle. Just a matter of remembering why I'm here and connecting the dots, and it's all right there.

As I mentioned earlier, I didn't want this book to be an ancestry research journal, so I gave you an abridged version of these years. There was the short break I took to do a tour in the Navy. Not my favorite experience, but it helped me realize a lot more just how special my Father's Naval career was. And just F.Y.I., there was no break from the drug scene there either. What my short, and not so sweet stint in the Navy did do for me though, was re-focus me on my passion at that time, which was dancing, and when I got out was when I got really serious about Locking, and my career took off.

As my dancing career came to a close, I sought the advice from a professional choreographer that had gotten me a lot of work over the years and asked her what my next move should be. She said, "Stay in shape, get an agent, and take some acting classes." I, of course, did not follow any of that advice. I did, however, accept a job from her husband. He was a well-known producer/director, and at the time had a popular T.V. show currently airing. This job was not in the entertainment field, or at least not as you would think.

He also owned a private investigations company. They specialized in finding run-aways of the rich, and famous. He knew that most of the missing run-aways of his clients were on the streets of Hollywood. He also knew with my credible street experience, the way I looked, and having my own issues with drug addiction, I could easily infiltrate that world. After some training, I was off. I have always known of the existence of demons, but it wasn't until I was out in the field looking for these run-aways that I for the first time came face to face with the demonic!

To this day whenever I pass by a so-called homeless town, and Las Vegas has some huge ones, including a whole other world under the city in the sewer system, and underground tunnels. I know it's because of an experience I had while working the streets as to why I'm not downtown more often getting my preach on or handing out food, etc. I had a couple of kids on the streets I could go to, and get information from as to the whereabouts of certain run-aways I was trying to find. One particular run-away of extreme importance was rumored to be hanging around this particular area of downtown Los Angeles.

Here I am by myself in a homeless town at 4:00 A.M. in the morning, yeah, I know! I find myself walking down an alley with a penlight, and a picture of this missing kid. I was just supposed to make a positive I.D., and call it in. A retrieval team would follow up. There are a half dozen or so people lying on the ground up against the sides of the alley. I slowly, and quietly work my way, side to side, back, and forth, trying to make a positive I.D., and not be too intrusive. I eventually get to the end of the alley, and there's no exit, it's a dead end. I turn around to start heading back the other way and came face to face with a bunch of these people who just a moment ago were sleeping, and now they are all up, bunched together in the middle of the alley, every one of them crouched down on all fours. I cannot make out any faces, it's dark in the alley, and I aim my penlight at them, and it doesn't work. Then they all start growling at me like a bunch of wild dogs. I am so unable to wrap my mind around what is happening, I'm frozen with fear. When they all start to slowly crawl toward me, I collapse onto my ass, I bring my knees to my chest, I hug my legs, and lower my face into my chest, and I began to pray.

    I don't recall any particular prayer(s), I do recall just talking to God as though He's hovering above me watching this situation unfold, and speaking to Him in plain English, and asking for His intervention.

As I sit there with my eyes closed, the growling is louder, and getting louder, and I have the overwhelming feeling I'm about to get pounced on! All of a sudden it's dead silent. I mean dead silent! I'm expecting an explosion of pain, but it doesn't come. Then a welcome sense of calm comes over me. I hear someone clear their throat. I open my eyes, look up, and standing over me looking down at me with a smile on his face is a person I don't know, but he knows me. He says, "Shawn", and holds out his hand. I was never so happy to see someone from the retrieval team before.

I take his hand, and get to my feet. I just wanted to get out of there. It doesn't even occur to me to tell this guy what just happened, I just want to get out of there. As we walk down the alley side by side, I notice all of the people in the alley are back where they were at, on the sides of the alley, but each and everyone of them are down in the upright fetal position, on their elbows and knees, and hiding their faces. As we continue down the alley, I glance over at this guy I've never met before, and it's possible that the street lights were hitting him just right, because he appeared in the darkness to have a very ever so slight glow to him. We get to the end of the alley, I point one way and say my car's over there. He smiles, turns in the other direction, and walks off. I didn't say another word, got into my car, and drove home.

The following day I get a call from the job. It's my boss, and he wants to know if I made an I.D., and why I didn't check in?! I said, "Didn't your guy from the retrieval team fill you in on what happened?"

The boss says, "What guy, from where?"

I said, "The guy you sent out that found me and got me out of a jam."

The boss says, "I had no one from any of the retrieval teams working last night". He went on to say that he would have sent someone out if I had made a positive I.D., checked in, and called for a team. He added that I was the only one working the streets for him the night before!

I have given this a lot of thought over many years, and I have a pretty good idea who I think it was, and if I'm right, I'll get another chance one day to thank him. I can't wait!! Well, I value your opinions, who do you all think he was?!!!!!......

That was the last case I worked for that company. I bounced around from job to job in Los Angeles, while still struggling with addiction. I know what's it gonna take right? So many plans and dreams for my career, and future in Los Angeles, but it just wasn't meant to be. I never stopped being Catholic, but one good thing did come out of this, I did come back more to my religion, and got stronger in my faith again. I never stopped praying for God to help me with my addictions, and to show me the way. He showed me alright, all the way to Las Vegas, Nevada. What a haunted roller coaster ride it has been, and continues to be for me in Las Vegas.

Las Vegas, Nevada is one of the most, if not the most haunted town I have ever lived in!

I have experienced everything in Las Vegas, ghosts, non-human entities, shadow figures, poltergeists, malevolent spirits, dopplegangers, and demons!!! I have also experienced the Holy Spirit, Angels, and have been on the receiving side of extreme divine intervention here too in Las Vegas. You ready, grab your holy water, crucifix, and Bible, you're Headed to Las Vegas, your tour guide, "The Rev".

6

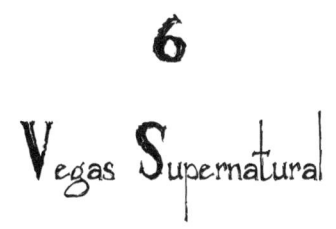

Vegas Supernatural

As I'm writing this, it has been 16 years since I met, fell in love with, and married my wife, Sharon. Sharon is a Stephen Minister in the Lutheran Church, and we co-founded Ghost-B-Gone.biz (the ministry). It has been going strong for that stretch of time. For many years prior, I was a lone wolf paranormal investigator. I worked many cases, but I don't want to bore you. I will though share one case that even today is one of the strangest I've ever encountered.

I like to call this case, "The Killer Orbs", very controversial. Some people love them while others find them boring, or claim they are all dust. I'm sorry brothers and sisters, but I know orbs are not very exciting. They just so happen to be the way many spirit energies appear when they manifest, boring or not?! My friend, Stan, a former co-worker, and close friend for many years, and our interests at the time were mostly girls and partying, but he was aware of my side passion as a paranormal authority.

He tells me this tale of this yellow, orange, reddish glowing ball of energy ranging in size from a softball to a soccer ball that would appear to him, every few days. This could happen anywhere, in his truck, his home, at the movies, a nightclub, wherever! When this orb appeared it would psychically relay the message to him that in no uncertain terms, it was going to have his soul. This eventually escalated to attacks while he slept. He would wake up out of a dead sleep with this orb hovering over him. Before he could react it would disappear right into his chest.

He explained the pain being like holding onto a small piece of metal, and jamming it into a light socket, and not letting go while a Volkswagen bug was parked on his chest, totally paralyzing him.

His parents were church going folk, and Dad was a retired cop. Stan was a good guy, not into anything creepy?! I honestly did not know how to advise him. One night after having been out on the town until the wee hours, I invited Stan to come crash on my couch. I wasn't asleep long, and woke to what sounded like Stan having a stroke in my living room. I ran into my living room, and saw a red glowing energy ball the size of a bowling ball suspended in air over Stan's chest, while he lay on my couch struggling to breathe. This ball then sank down, and disappeared right into Stan's chest. He reacted violently to this, and then became eerily still. His body then appeared to arch backward, and he levitated up off my couch about a foot into the air. I ran back into my bedroom, and grabbed a crucifix and some holy water.

I approached my friend, put the crucifix on his stomach, and continually kept splashing him with holy water. This orb exited, and re-entered my friend 2 or 3 times until settling back in him, and it for a moment seemed as though he did have a car parked on top of him, the way he sank down into the sofa cushions. True fear came over me when for a moment he appeared dead. So still!! I put the crucifix on his chest, and poured holy water on his head, and began to pray. If I said the Hail Mary once, I said it 25 times followed by Our Fathers.

This thing eventually rose up out of my friend, hovered for a moment, then shot up and out through my ceiling. After a pot of coffee and a couple of hot pockets, we discussed my friend's next move. Stan's parents did not believe in this entity, and Stan was in between jobs, and hated Las Vegas. So we decided he should move back to Los Angeles, move in with his older brother until he got on his feet, and re-invented himself. I did get him to commit to me to start going back to Confession, Mass, and Communion every week from that point on in L.A. He agreed, and has kept his word. I'm happy to announce he now lives an "orb free" life and has not come under attack or seen that anomaly again! Yeah, orbs are just boring dust!!!

Haunted objects, another controversial subject. A girl (friend) of mine told me her family had a cursed haunted pillow. That's right, and I'm not talking one of those my favorite pillows you see on T.V. This was an old, old down feather pillow that had been in her family for many, many years. At least 2 or more family members over the years had actually passed away while resting and laying their heads on this pillow. No one in the family seemed to know where this pillow originally came from. They claimed that when you slept on the pillow, you would hear voices. They wanted me to experience this phenomena, and then come up with a solution as to what to do with the pillow. I took the pillow home, and don't say, I know, I slept on it! And, as I sit here writing this, I have to tell you, that night I did experience what sounded like several people chanting in the pillow. Very creepy indeed! I gave the pillow the once over checking for a hidden audio device of any kind, and nothing. I then realized I was starting to entertain some very ugly thoughts, very ugly. I put the pillow on top of my living room table, and waited. My great dane at the time, a dog that feared nothing, got up, looked at the pillow, began to growl, and with tail tucked went to hide in the master bedroom.

A short time later, I heard the trash truck pull up outside. I grabbed the pillow, walked downstairs, and with one hand gave a $ 20.00 dollar bill to the garbage man, and with the other hand threw the pillow into the back of the trash truck. I winked at the garbage man, and walked back inside my home. My friend's family was quite upset I got rid of the pillow without discussing it with them first. My response was, "Bill me." So, haunted and cursed objects, it's a very real thing. Be careful buying old clothing from thrift stores! Be cautious when purchasing religious relics, antiques, old items at yard sales, and accepting any hand me downs of any kind from friends or people you don't know. Now that I think about it, I may have a cursed pair or two of underwear, just sayin?!

Well, brothers and sisters, this is where the journey gets much darker, and takes an unexpected turn. The Ghost-B-Gone.biz early years. Just a lot of fun for the most part. Sharon and I like taking long drives on our days off to travel around Southern Nevada with no particular destination in mind. We would stop at every old abandoned shack, structure, or old West cemetery to explore, and take photos.

Over the years after Sharon and I got married, those close to us knew of our interest in the paranormal, and from time to time friends and friends of friends would approach us with their own paranormal issues, and if they needed our help and asked for it, we would always try to oblige them. Always pretty straight forward stuff like a spirit remaining in a home they died in, and when new tenants moved in, the presence made itself known to them. Or Aunt Betty, or Uncle Bob hanging around watching over their loved ones.

Then there was Cece. Cece was a co-worker of mine who heard through the grapevine that I did the ghost thing, and came to me for advice. She claimed that some unseen force was raping her at night while she slept next to her husband. Whenever the husband would witness this, he would write it off as seizures until he tried to intervene, and got attacked himself. The frequency of the attacks increased, in both how often it happened, and in severity. She wasn't safe anywhere, kitchen, shower, or even the 2nd floor balcony. Honestly, Sharon and I had never worked a case like this before, and we were a bit apprehensive. Looking back, perhaps it would have been better to have passed on this, I guess you could call it opportunity, but we took it on, and it changed our lives forever!

Our first time at Cece's in the daytime, I walked into her living room, and began filming with an ordinary camcorder. As I panned across the living room, I saw on the view finder what appeared to be for lack of a better description, an angel standing in the middle of the room. I looked up, and this was not visible to the naked eye. As I would pan the camera off that spot, it was gone, but when I panned back, it re-appeared. I got the brilliant idea to walk through this anomaly. As I did this my body got quite a jolt. An electrical charge of some sort. All the hair on my head stood straight out, and I had difficulty catching my breath. I turned around, and the anomaly was still not visible to me, but still appeared on my camera's view finder. So, I walked right back into this whatever it was, yeah, I know?!

Same reaction, except this time my camera blew up. Not literally, but I heard a loud pop, and my camera began to smoke, and it was done, it wouldn't work at all after that. I remember my wife taking the camera back to where she bought it, and the salesman asked her if the camera had been in a fire. Our first visit to Cece's wasn't very productive, as all our equipment kept malfunctioning. Sharon, who is a two time near-death experience survivor that came back from those experiences with an extreme sensitivity to spirit, commented that whatever was there gave her feelings like she had never had before, same with me. We did briefly entertain thoughts of passing this case onto another team, but we realized Cece really needed help, and she came to me as a friend. We had no clue what we were up against and had no idea what we were about to come face to face with.

Our second, and last visit to Cece's was at night, and one we will never forget. Much of the same ole' thing, malfunctioning equipment, but a lot of personal experiences. This would also be the first, and last time I ever did any provoking of a spirit or entity. Everyone was sitting at different parts in the living room. I was at the living room table, and Cece and her husband were on the other side of the room sitting on a couch.

I remember demanding this entity to give us a sign of its presence. On command, it sounded like a large man with a huge club or baseball bat, smacked the wall behind the young married couple, causing them to launch straight up in the air about a foot high, and land straight back down, and they just stared at me like deers in the headlights! I said to them, "Did you hear that?" what a dumb question, they just nodded yes, but never uttered a word. Then, if that wasn't bad enough, I came up with another brilliant idea to have a séance right there, and then, and got out my Ouija board.

The séance was actually pretty non-productive. After a short period of time trying to make some kind of contact with something, we all heard a disembodied voice of a woman call out Cece's name, and then say, "Stop now." We took that as a sign to stop the séance, so we did just that. Sharon and I were tired and decided to pack up, and head home, and come back another day. As we left, little did we know that would be the last time we would see Cece. Sharon and I were about to go through our own ordeal. One that would challenge us like never before. We would find ourselves in a battle between life and death and go on a dark malevolent, and possibly demonic trip through several cases in a row that also took us on a personal tour of hell!

The story I'm about to share with you is one unlike any you have read about before, and unlike one that you may have experienced or like anything anyone you know of in this field has ever gone through, I promise you. Although I have laid hands on, and said many prayers of protection, and deliverance over my writings, I cannot promise you that some negative energy is not conjured up by talking about such things. I implore you to please take caution as you read on.

7
Home Is Where The Heart Is

It's 3:00 a.m. in the morning. It's always 3:00 a.m. in the morning when the most unexplainable paranormally charged incidents happen, right?! My wife and I are driving home from the house of our then current client, who has an unseen force sexually molesting her. Sharon's cell phone starts ringing, but no number appears in the caller I.D. I naturally assumed it was our client, and told Sharon to answer it. She answered the phone, and no one was there. I didn't think much of it and drove home.

Everything seemed to be fine when we arrived home. We were exhausted, and quickly got ready for bed, and retired for the evening. I was only in bed for about an hour, and maybe fell asleep for 15 minutes, when I had a strange dream. I wouldn't categorize the dream as a night terror, but it was odd, to say the least. I dreamt a large black mass, or black cloud was hovering over me at the ceiling while I lay in bed. As I stared at this mass, it begins to quickly swoop down upon me, and stop just short of hitting my face, then quickly raised back up to the ceiling. It repeats this behavior 2 or 3 times until I all of a sudden wake-up, and there's nothing there. I wasn't frightened, but considering everything I had been through that evening, I couldn't get back to sleep, so I sat up in bed, and watched some T.V., on low volume so as not to wake up Sharon.

    The next day while sitting in my kitchen, I heard children playing in my garage. I was convinced I left my garage door open, and some neighborhood kids were in my garage. I went out there, and nothing. No kids and the garage door was shut and locked. A little later that day, I went out into my front yard to do some yard work. I noticed there were two large black birds perched on the eave of my roof just above my front door. I began to wonder just what kind of birds they were, not crows nor ravens, unlike any type of bird I had seen in Southern Nevada. I started doing some gardening, and suddenly these two birds started dive bombing me. You see this happen to people, and it's funny, but when it happens to you, especially when they are hitting you in the head, and coming at your face relentlessly, not funny at all. I ran inside a bit freaked out.

    A short time later, there it is again, sounds like children playing in my garage. I go out there, and to my amazement, and shock, there is a large swarm of bees flying around in my garage. I panic and immediately shut my kitchen door. Now, I'm really freaked. What is going through my mind is, I can't afford a bee specialist to come out, and get rid of the bees, and I can't just leave them in my garage. OK, what is my next move. I decided to make myself a makeshift bee suit, go into my garage through the kitchen, walk slowly over to the garage door, unlock it, and slowly walk back into the house. The one thing I don't want to do is walk out there flailing my arms around. It would be just my luck they would be African bees, and this story would end with me running down the street with a swarm of bees chasing me screaming, and looking for a pool to jump in, which is not the thing to do, so it wouldn't end well at all.

    I execute my plan to the tee, and I end up back in my house waiting to see what happens. A couple of hours later, I look into my garage and thank you, Jesus, the bees are gone! I remember asking out loud, OK, what next?! I had no idea, and no reason to think this day would end, and I would have a couple of odd but funny stories to tell. Little did I know I was in for a long, long night. A relatively uneventful evening to start, but Sharon goes to bed, and I stay up to watch a little late night T.V. 11:00 P.M. rolls around, and I hear what sounds like my cat being ripped apart by wild dogs in my back yard. I have an outdoor cat, and there are plenty of loose dogs running around in the neighborhood, so I launch out of my chair, and grab a bat, and a flashlight, and run outside. I'm standing on my back porch staring at some bushes in my back yard just a few feet away from me, and some kind of animal is being attacked by other animals, and I'm shining my light right at the bushes, and I can't see anything. My heart is pounding, and I'm shaking, and I'm convinced it has to be a cat fight because how could dogs get into my fenced off backyard. Then as quickly as it started, it's now dead silent. I run out front and find my cat sound asleep in her cat home out front. I'm relieved, but now totally freaked. I go back to watching T.V., and when I'm just about to call it a night, it's around 12:30 A.M., I hear what sounds like a condor, do they even have condors in Nevada, or maybe it was as pterodactyl?! Whatever it was, it sounded like it was wearing combat boots, as it ran from one end of my roof to the other, then crashing through my roof into my attic! IF you asked 20 people what they would do next, you would get 20 different answers. I was frozen to my seat and shaking like a leaf on a tree. Fearing for my wife, and my dogs, I grabbed a step ladder, went into the master bedroom closet, climbed upon the ladder, popped the hatch to the attic, and looked in, only to find no creature in my attic or hole in my roof.

I was sober but decided to pour myself a strong whiskey and coke to settle my nerves, and the best thing was to try and get some sleep. Obviously, I was overtired.

I probably wasn't asleep longer than an hour or so, when I had the same dream as before with the hovering black mass. This time the dream seemed more intense, and it actually launched me out of bed, and I stepped into ankle deep water. The room was flooded, and water was gushing out of the wall. I ran outside and turned the water main off.

Apparently, a water pipe in our wall had burst, and flooded us out of the master bedroom.

We had to end up sleeping in the living room on the floor for a few days while the plumber and flood clean up people did their thing. The plumbing was fixed first, but because of some drywall and carpet damage, we had to wait until things dried out in the master bedroom. Over the next couple of weeks, I began to have a variety of night terrors, and still experienced the phantom animal attacks out back, and the creature landing on my roof. I finally realized there was something wrong when religious items in my home would come up missing, and one of my Bibles was found chewed up in the master bedroom. The room was blocked off because repairs were being done, so I couldn't blame the Bible incident on my dogs. I recall one evening while taking the trash out, I saw what appeared to be a solid, three dimensional human figure, all black standing by a tree, and when I saw it, it tried to hide behind the tree, but the tree was much thinner than the figure, and I realized the figure just vanished. I called my client up to check on her because with everything going on, I kind of forgot about her. My client told me that since Sharon and I were last there at her house, things really have calmed down at her place. It then hit me like a bolt of lightning, something had followed us home!

    I had absolutely no clue how to deal with this so I put the word out into the paranormal community for help, and I'm happy to say help did come my way. I was introduced to a person who would become my mentor for a while. This person was an exorcist who took me under their wing and showed me step by step what I needed to do, and get this thing to move on. It didn't happen overnight, but this thing in my home did move on, but to where?

I had been so consumed with getting this thing to move out of my house and to get my life and home back, I didn't realize just what a toll it had taken on my wife, Sharon. Sharon at this time was the strongest and healthiest person I knew. She didn't drink or smoke, or have any history of cancer in her family.

Sharon is a two time near-death experience survivor. The first time she was for a moment pronounced dead after having a severe asthma attack when she was young. To this day she clearly remembers crossing over to heaven, seeing all her family, and relatives that crossed over before, and just how beautiful heaven is! She heard a voice say, "It's not your time," and she was shot back down into her body, and revived.

She came back from that experience with an extreme sensitivity to spirit and was a real magnet from that time on for paranormal activity. I refer to her as my human dowsing rod, and she is invaluable to me on paranormal investigations.

We were unaware at this time, we were about to be drug through hell, because of our ordeal here in the home, and she was about to come face to face with her second near-death experience. I did notice that Sharon started to have night terrors too. She would start groaning and moaning loud while she slept. This would, of course, send the dogs, and me launching out of bed. Most times she would just fall back asleep, and other times she would sleepwalk. I would always stop her, and help her back in bed.

One morning I get into my car, and head to work. While driving, I absolutely saw one of those same shadow figures I've seen around my property, sitting in my back seat in the rear view mirror. I whipped my head around a couple of times, and even pulled over so I could completely turn around, and look. I was absolutely positive something or someone was there, I just couldn't see it. I continued on to work as usual. It was comforting that I did not have that same feeling in my car on the way home from work.

A few days passed with the unexplainable odd occurrences still happening at the house. I was still in constant contact with my mentor, and the offer was made to me to continue to further my training in regards to dealing with such matters. It was the first time I heard the term spiritual warfare. I began my training through a Christian University, and An Association of Exorcists.

It wasn't long before I began to hear co-workers at my job talking about and discussing paranormal activity. I learned a long time ago to wait for people to ask for your help. I knew everyone knew me as "the ghost guy" so I decided to take a wait, and see approach.

With everything that I had recently been through, I couldn't help but think that something had, in fact, followed me to work. Well, do you think that is what happened?

Next thing I know, management at work approached me, and requested I come there one night, and conduct an investigation. Things had escalated fast, and the night crew was scared to work. The night Sharon and I did the investigation at work, we did capture some evidence, and had plenty of personal experiences. Whatever was there wouldn't leave Sharon alone. I remember on our way home that night Sharon commented that she just didn't feel right.

A couple of days later, Sharon came home from work early which was odd, and claimed she wasn't feeling well. As she is telling me this, she sounds as though she is drunk, or having a stroke. She told me she broke a tooth, and her tongue was scraping against it. She had already made an appointment to see her dentist. By the time she saw the dentist, only a few days had passed, and she was then only able to eat very soft food, and even that was a chore. The dentist took one look, and said that it's not your tooth, it's your tongue, and I'm sending you to an Ear, Nose, and Throat specialist as soon as possible!

Next day or so, the specialist took one look and said that it's a rare form of tongue cancer called Squamous Cell Carcinoma.

At this time, Sharon couldn't talk, and couldn't even swallow water. The Ear, Nose, and Throat Doctor rushed her to the hospital to have a feeding tube put in, which she had for over a year. She then went through 35 straight days of high doses of radiation treatments in her mouth, neck, and collar bone area. She looked like a severe burn victim with the world's worst ever sunburn on her face and neck. The skin was just peeling off, and she had the smell of death about her too. The Doctors also put her through 8 weeks of high doses of chemotherapy. Complete hair loss, and severe nausea every day all day long for 6 weeks until they decided to discontinue chemotherapy because it was killing her. Imagine this, she can't even swallow, so what do you think vomiting was like?

In a matter of weeks, she went from 127 pounds to 93 pounds. At that point, she was admitted into the hospital, and put into the isolation ward. I went to sleep alongside Sharon many a night expecting to wake up beside her, only to find her dead. We didn't find out until much later that all the Doctors working with her didn't expect her to live. They wanted to send her to UCLA to have her tongue removed, her reply was, "No way, I'll have to die then!"

Why am I telling you all this, what does this have to do with the paranormal? Sharon didn't drink or smoke, and had no history of cancer in her family. I received a phone call one night from a childhood buddy that was clear on the other side of the country, on his deathbed, from advanced colon cancer. I knew that my friend had very little faith, if any, and was not a religious person. He told me that God came to him in a dream, and told him Sharon was not going to die, and for me to continue to fight those responsible, and that our battle was far from over. How right he was because shortly after that Sharon was diagnosed with a rare form of thyroid cancer called, Medullary Cancer.

No cure for it, and it tends to spread, which it did to lymph nodes in her neck in addition to her thyroid. So, an operation to remove her thyroid, and several lymph nodes, and we're as good as gold! I decided then, fighting those responsible would have to wait, and I took a year off of the paranormal cases to help my wife fight for her life.

Can I prove the demonic were responsible for Sharon's illness, NO. But, what I can tell you is, it is because of extreme divine intervention Sharon is still here, and it's been over 5 years now. I did many a night, go to an all-night prayer chapel, and crawled on my hands and knees to the altar, and petitioned to God on Sharon's behalf to please spare her life in the name of his Son, Jesus Christ!!

I decided while on my sabbatical from the paranormal I would continue my schooling in the field of Spiritual Warfare with the intention of getting ordained, God willing. There is no rest for the weary though, we are still battling issues with Sharon's illness because these disgusting creatures are like paranormal gangsters, they go after what you love, and therefore she will always be a target. Is this all starting to make sense now, I certainly hope so.

I learned how to properly bless my property and home, and seal up my home against invading unclean spirits, but even then, and throughout the time I took off to become ordained, the drive-bys continued, including the paranormal activity at the workplace.

8
They Run In A Pack

There's an old saying, in God's time, if it is God's will. Let me start by saying, I never did nor do I have any aspiration to be on T.V. I'm not a big fan of the reality paranormal T.V. shows, mainly because they're not reality. And, I know I could never truly get my message out there on T.V. It's sad, but God doesn't provide good ratings. I take that back in some venues yes, but not in a paranormal reality (not) T.V. show! Having said that, I get a phone call from my mentor, and I'm asked if I would like to be a part of an exorcism team for a new reality show on a major network.

Ordinarily, I would have said no, but this was someone I trusted, and I decided if it was good enough for them, it was meant to be. I said yes because Sharon and I were so financially devastated from fighting her cancer that I thought this could be life-changing. Everything was a go, green-lighted by the network, and I had just gotten ordained, so I was ready. Right before filming started, my mentor came down with a rare life-threatening disease, and had to retire. The show was over before it began. It wasn't God's time or will, and perhaps other forces were behind my mentor's illness.

I knew that having become ordained, something that I could feel made my Mother and Father in Heaven very happy, and I was about to embark on another even more important journey. Before I could ask, God, what's next, a former co-worker of mine named Lacy reached out to me with a very eye-opening tale. She had quit her job where I was still working months prior because she really felt targeted by an unseen force at work. She now was convinced whatever this was, had attached itself to her, and she brought it home to her family. She was a single Mother with three kids, and her elderly Mother living with them.

Her oldest Son had Downs Syndrome and was totally non-verbal. He was waking in the middle of the night screaming as if something was after him, and he would wander out into the hallway with a blanket, and sleep there rather than stay in his room. Her second oldest Son and Daughter both were being affected too. Her Daughter was seeing spirits as was Mom and her second oldest claimed a shadow figure appeared to him in his closet and asked him if he believed in God.

Sharon was doing a little better, but still struggling. She is very stubborn and refused to let me work this case alone, so she came with me on our first visit there. By this time I have to come to realize that my gift of discernment is that I can hear and see demons. Some might call it a curse, I know beyond a shadow of a doubt, it's an absolute gift from God and one that I couldn't do without in my calling to this ministry! We pull up to Lacy's house, and its high noon in Las Vegas, hot and sunny, but the house appears to me from the outside as though I'm looking at it through sunglasses. I already knew that this meant the house was already experiencing a demonic infestation. I had no idea of the degree or severity of it at this point. My plan was to have the whole family in one area downstairs, and while Sharon tried to comfort them, would interview them at the same time.

While I, on my own, went through the home with my video camera rolling, and do a walk-through to see what I might see, and feel what I might feel. In this field, we are not so concerned about capturing evidence as we are just wanting to help the family. Some in this field like to provoke, I'm not a big fan of that approach, especially if there are young children present. I have found that just my presence in a home where a malevolent entity is present is provocation enough.

As I walked through the house, I looked for writing on the walls or furniture that might indicate occult practices being performed in the home.

I never mentioned this to the Mother, but I did observe some odd writings (symbols) in the garage on the walls. Relatively non-productive walk through after that until I got into the master bedroom closet. I grabbed a stepladder and positioned it under the attic hatch. I began to lift up the hatch so I could take a peek into the crawl space, and I only lifted it up about a foot or so, and all of a sudden it felt like someone was in the crawl space, and the person stomped down on the hatch causing it to crash down on my head hard enough to make me drop my camera, and I felt dizzy for a moment. AH-HA, I found you, I thought to myself!

Then before I had a chance to figure out my next move, something actually put its hand on my shoulder firmly and physically escorted me out of the bedroom. As soon as I was pushed through the bedroom door, and was out on the landing at the top of the stairs, and this thing let me go, the bedroom door slammed! The Mother yelled up to me from downstairs, "You ok?"

I replied, "Yes, sorry, didn't mean to slam the door." I'm not going to lie to you, yes I was quite shaken, but I decided to sit down on a chair close by and record a testimonial about what just happened. Shortly after that, Sharon and I left so we could discuss our feelings, and re-group so to speak. Several days passed by, and I was in constant contact with the Mother. Things apparently had escalated, and Sharon and I decided to go back the following weekend, this time at night.

Sometimes little things happen that at first, your mind writes them off as nothing. Then later you realize, hey, wait a minute, that was a sign, or something meant for me?! I'm referring to us walking up to the front door, and before I even knock, the front porch light begins to flicker, and Sharon says, "Do you smell that, smells like a skunk died in her yard?" I walked around the property and could find no skunk or sewer issues.

The Mother confirmed not having any issues with her sewage, and maybe it was a dead animal. We were out in the middle of the desert up against some hills in a new housing tract, could be nothing right? I know I'm a weirdo, and some of my methods are beyond outside the box, and I do get into trouble with my mentor, and others in this field, but when you have been doing this as long as I have, you learn a few things. There are some techniques I practice when I'm alone in another part of the house without the client's looking so they don't think I'm a complete basket case.

Like wearing a really nice expensive pair of stethoscopes, and putting the listening end up against a wall. You would be amazed at what you might actually pick up doing this. On this visit we planned on just doing a quick walk-through, taking some photos, and then doing a cleansing, and blessing of the home and property. As soon as I got to the top of the stairs, and out of the view of everyone downstairs, I put on the stethoscope and applied the tip to a wall. I was shocked to hear what sounded like an actual heartbeat with the intermittent moan by something. I quickly decided enough with the walk-through, get to the blessing. I turned to go downstairs, and there was the client's daughter standing in the doorway of the master bedroom. I asked her, "Honey what are you doing up here, I need everyone downstairs." She didn't answer me, she just kept staring at me, and then I got hit with a frigid blast of icy cold air, and that same smell I smelled outside when we arrived. I realized I wasn't looking at the daughter. I quickly pulled out my holy water, and began flailing holy water in the sign of the cross at this apparition!

In the blink of an eye this apparition turns into what can best be described as a small feral cat, a pig-like creature which runs right at me, then past me into one of the bedrooms, up onto a bed, then out a second story window! I had to sit down on the floor with my back against the wall, and think about that one for a while.

I sat there praying, and heard a voice say, "Finish what you came here to do," so I did. I used all the weapons I had brought with me, holy water, holy oil, blessed chalk, blessed sea, and kosher salt, blessed frankincense, and left a few blessed religious items displayed around the home. So, what is the common denominator here, everything I used was blessed, and I recited the strongest prayers of deliverance, and exorcism available to me in every room, including closets, garage crawl space above. I only used the incense, holy water, and prayer outside, but I buried a St. Michael and St. Benedict medal in the ground on the four corners of the property! The medals were blessed too!! Things did calm down quite a bit for this family over the weeks ahead. The family did decide on their own to move. Eventually, when they called I felt it was my job to support their decision when it is their decision. I would never advise a family to move unless it is a last resort. My motto has always been, "Draw your line in the sand, make your stand, and fight back, and keep on fighting no matter what." This family was also Christian and Catholic, and totally on board with me and my approach which is an absolute necessity.

I did capture a photo of what appeared to be a large heavy set person, no head, no hands or feet, floating across the upstairs landing. This is one of those times where you walk a fine line between what you should or shouldn't share with your client. This time I decided to share. When Lacy saw this photo, she fainted!

Looking back, this photo along with a few other things probably played a big part in her deciding to relocate her family. So, if you're a paranormal investigator reading this, trust me there will be times when you have to make a hard decision on what you should or shouldn't share with your client. There have been things I have been told by demons as to what they were going to do to a family if I didn't walk away.

I, of course, did not share such things, because your clients are already hanging on emotionally by their fingernails, and you do not want to contribute to the hysteria if you can help it.

I wasn't done with Lacy yet, or I should say she wasn't done with me yet. A short time later, she reached out to me and shared with me that she had concerns that whatever was at her home has now attached itself to her new boss at her new job. Her new boss even agreed that she was having some issues, and agreed to have Lacy reach out to me for her. Lacy's boss was a very nice woman, a Doctor named Karla. Karla did mention that her issues did indeed start shortly after hiring Lacy. Karla said that she began having a dream in which she would see a dark cloaked figure standing on the end of her bed staring down at her. Because she is seeing herself lying in bed, I have to ask, "Are you sure you're dreaming when you see this?", and she says that yes because after the little creature that accompanies this figure bites me, I launch out of bed screaming, and always profusely sweating, and then there's this, and she shows me these bite marks on her arms. That quite frankly is very sobering to look at, and they all appeared infected, even though she has been trying to take care of them. She tells me that this figure at the foot of her bed doesn't speak, it just looks at her, points at her then points at a black pit in the middle of "HER ROOM."

    I can't seem to take my eyes off her bite wounds, and I ask, "What exactly are we talking here that bit you?" She says that it looks like an ugly mangy possum on steroids with rabies!

I immediately say, "Could this creature also pass for a feral cat, pig-like creature?"

She gives me a wide-eyed glance, and says "Absolutely!" Okay, brothers and sisters, is this starting to sound familiar? She also started having seizures for the first time in her life. She had seen a couple of Doctors and had tests run, but they cannot figure out what is causing the seizures.

I could not make a judgment call then, but I suspected these weren't seizures at all. She added that she had to lie to her Doctor about the bites because she didn't want him to think she was crazy. According to Karla, she told the Doctor one of her outdoor cats that's really big, and part wild doesn't like her and bit her when she tried to pick it up. She said his response was, "That must be one fucking big ass pissed off cat!!! You should really get rid of it." I'm not going to lie, I got a good laugh out of that, and forgive me Jesus for cussing. This is an ugly business we're in, and you have to find the humor where you can, or you do go a little bit s!#t crazy...

It just so happens that while we are having this conversation with Karla, she yells out, "OUCH!" She holds her arm up, and right in front of my eyes appears this large red welt that begins to bleed as holes appear where the skin has been ripped away, and it looks like she just got bitten by a large animal! This sort of occurrence never ceases to shock everyone that witnesses it.

Karla then says that she doesn't feel right, and needs to sit down. We walk her into the living room and sit her down in a lounge chair. Then she begins to have one of these seizures. My suspicions are quickly confirmed when the seizures are accompanied by an ice cold, and I mean ice cold breeze, and a bad, bad odor.

Now everyone seems to use the term burning sulfur when describing this demonic smell. Yes, burning sulfur can be used to describe one of these odors. The smell of the demonic is "DEATH," and death comes in many different levels. I have experienced what smelled like someone with really bad gas, to extremely rancid meat, to the burning sulfur, to a mixture of vomit and diarrhea in a bucket, and splashes into your face. This smell goes right into your nostrils, and down your throat, and you can't shake it.

That's why many times you will witness an exorcist vomit in the presence of the demonic.

Karla loses consciousness, her eyes roll back, and she begins to flail, and shake as though she is being electrocuted to death. It took everything for three grown people, Sharon, myself, and another team member to hold Karla down. I look up to see this black mist or fog start to develop above us. I instruct Sharon, and my other team member to hold on tight, and no matter what, don't let go. I stood up, and poured holy water in my right hand, and started touching Karla on different parts of her body making the sign of the cross with my palm, and a lot of holy water. I'm now actually pouring holy water onto her head and running my fingers, which are drenched in holy water, through her hair. I watch this black mist slowly lower and enter into Karla's body through her chest. I stand up, straight up, and begin to yell out loud something to the effect of, "I command you unclean spirit to leave this child of God, and go straight to the foot of the cross for Jesus to deal with you!" over and over again. It got eerily quiet, and all of a sudden this black mist rises up out of Karla, and shoots right in, then out of my back. I spin around, and come face to face with a solid three-dimensional shadow figure!

To me they don't look like a shadow, they appear as a solid human figure that has been dipped in black tar! No facial features and no visible genitalia to determine male or female. This figure slowly turns around and begins to walk down the hallway leading to the master bedroom.

Earlier upon our arrival, during our initial walk-through I had positioned a large metal ladder in the master bedroom closet leading up, and into the crawl space above.

I turned to Sharon, and my other team member, and said to keep holding Karla, don't let go of her, I'll be right back, and I turned to follow the dark figure down the hall!

I can see this figure turn, and go into the master bedroom. I'm almost to the bedroom door, and I can audibly hear someone climbing up the ladder in the closet.

I'll admit it, standing at the bottom of that ladder, looking up into this black hole in the ceiling, and debating whether or not to climb that ladder, I almost just called it a day, but next thing I know I'm climbing this ladder. Now listen carefully, this might save your life one day. I get to the top of the ladder and slowly poke my head up into the crawl space. I come face to face with this black figure which is crouched down on all fours, looking right at me about a foot from my face. It spits on my face and scurries off. This black ooze it spits on me is all over my face and glasses. Thank God I had my glasses on, and thank-you Jesus, I had my mouth closed! I would come to label this substance as demonic venom. You absolutely do not want to ingest this stuff. Those that I know who have become violently ill and some have died from it.

After this day, I made the judgment call that an exorcism was needed here. At this time I had not taken authority over an exorcism, or even assisted in one, so I had to call in the big guns. I assembled a team of a few of the most highly respected exorcists that I knew, and they began to make arrangements to come to Las Vegas. Some were driving, some were flying. Karla was a grown woman with no family, or relatives I needed to be concerned with. All I needed was her permission, which she gave freely.

The date for the exorcism was set about a week from then, and only a few days have passed, and I get a call from Lacy that Karla was gone! She upped and left her medical practice behind, packed up what she could fit in her truck, and was gone. I even contacted the police to file a missing person's report or amber alert, or something. The police told me that since Karla was a grown woman, and a professional, and there was no sign of a forced abduction, they couldn't do anything. We were also not blood relatives, so we didn't carry much weight. This is just one of the many heartbreaking aspects of this ministry.

    We really don't know exactly what these disgusting entities are capable of. Karla was convinced this thing that targeted her could also and did on a few occasions send her very nasty text messages in none other than Latin, that's right Latin! She tried to trace where these text messages originated from, even soliciting the help of her phone service, to no avail? You all will have to make your own judgment call on that one. I did though in fact see, and read some of them….

9
Man With No Face

They say there's no rest for the weary. I do indeed feel weary all the time, and I definitely don't get enough rest. That is what awaits those of you truly interested in becoming a paranormal investigator, a good one that is really passionate to help people. Here's my take if you have not been through a haunting whether it was your Aunt Bea, or Uncle Tom who is hanging around to watch over you, or a spirit of a person that died in the home you just moved into, and it doesn't want you there, to a non-human entity born from a tragedy on the land you live on, to God forbid a demonic presence in your home, you cannot possibly imagine what it is like to go through that!

It's okay to be a skeptic and try to debunk paranormal activity, but only in a business setting, or on a ghost hunt, but not in a residential setting where families are being affected, and are frightened. They need someone who's been there, done that, and someone who has a good bedside manner. Having said that, the last team member we had was with us at Karla's. The reason why now Ghost.B.Gone.biz is just Sharon and me is because the kind of cases we work now, we are too afraid for anyone else's safety. Shortly after Karla vanished our team member called me and said he felt something had attached itself to him, from Karla's house.

Rather quickly, he stopped wanting to eat, couldn't sleep, and when he did he would have night terrors. In addition to that, he was beginning to see things that made him feel he was going crazy. No, he didn't drink or smoke was not on prescription medication and was not suffering from mental illness. There is a terrible feeling of guilt when a friend is going through something like this, and you feel it's your fault for putting them in a dangerous situation.

We met one morning when he was on his way to work for coffee and to talk. I laid hands on him and prayed over him for a bit. He was Catholic, so it wasn't hard for me to convince him to start going back to confession, mass, and communion every week. I also suggested, not demanded but suggested that maybe he should consider saying goodbye to, and calling it a day with paranormal investigating, at least for a while. He agreed and headed on to work.

He called me later that night, and said, "Dude guess what, I think this thing left me and is now at my workplace. For the first time that day my office started to experience paranormal activity." I told him to stick with our plan for him, and to avoid getting caught up in what's going on there. We both said a prayer for his office, and co-workers, and hoped things would just work themselves out. Boy were we wrong. A few days later one of his co-workers that knew he did the ghost hunting came to him with some issues she was having at home.

Brothers and Sisters meet Anna. Start taking notes, this is where it gets really interesting to say the least. Anna is a single Mother with a young daughter with autism. Up to that time, Anna had never had any type of paranormal issues in her life, and her daughter wouldn't have any idea what that would be about. Her daughter also seemed up to this time, a very happy little girl, except for her condition. My friend took my advice, and just gave her my card, and tried to stay out of it.

When I first met Anna my impression of her was a good one. She had a really good head on her shoulders and loved her daughter to death. She also worked hard to try, and provide a better life for the two of them. Anna explained to me that she was more spiritual than religious, but she did believe in God and Jesus. She was a Christian. She was just living her life for her daughter, and trying to make the best of the situation, and trying to be the best version of herself on a day to day basis.

Anna claimed that the same day she experienced some odd unexplained things at work, she felt that something followed her home. That night, and two nights in a row back to back, she woke up out of a deep sleep to find her daughter, not in her bed. Both times she found her daughter in the dark, in the living room sitting straight up on the floor, legs straight out, facing the T.V., which was not turned on, in the dark! Both times she picked her daughter up, sat her down at the kitchen table, turned on a light, and asked her daughter, "What's wrong honey, are you OK?"

Both times her daughter said, "Mommy, Grandma is here, and she is trying to protect me from the man with no face." Here's the crazy thing, yeah it gets worse, Anna had never spoken about her Mother, her daughter's Grandmother, because Anna was not close with her Mother, and her Mother had passed years before her daughter was born. In tears, she begs me to come over. Now during this time, Sharon was still on quite the roller coaster ride with battling her cancer, so there were cases I passed on because she was too ill to go with me, or I would go by myself if I really felt it was the thing to do. This was one of those cases I worked by myself. I would also advise everyone in that field never to do that.

The night I went there, it was mid-evening. Anna wanted her daughter to be asleep when I got there. Anna's sister and nephew were there for support. I thought that was a good idea. I had everyone sitting in the living room as I did my walk-through. I quietly looked in on her daughter, and she seemed fine and was fast asleep. When I was in the master bedroom I really did feel like something was there, and that it really didn't want me there. You know when someone violently confronts you they are up in your bubble, your space, and right in your face, that even with your eyes closed you can feel their presence? That is how I felt no matter which way I turned or tried to walk, something was in my face. I slowly made my way back to the living room.

I was using a camera with night vision, so I had all the lights out, except for a candle burning on an end table next to the couch everyone was sitting on. My plan was to go back into the master bedroom, and take some holy water, and do a blessing. I did not want any of them to run into this thing, so I asked them all to please just stay where they were at. They had no problem with that. They were so scared as it was, they were all huddled up together on that couch, and were not moving. I took a couple more photos in the living room, put my camera down, grabbed my holy water, and headed down the hallway toward the master bedroom.

    About halfway down the hallway, I noticed what appeared to be someone standing in the master bedroom doorway. Too large to be the daughter, and actually not a human shape, just a much blacker area right in the middle of the doorway. A blackness much darker than the surrounding blackness. I'm not even able to take a moment to try and figure out what this is before it's on me. I don't remember a whole lot of what happened next, but what I do remember is I couldn't move, scream, or take in a big breath. All I could do is small rapid shallow breaths, and it felt like my heart was beating a mile a minute, and about to explode out of my chest. A pain beyond pain. I'm in the grasp of a giant who is slowly squeezing the life out of me while others are around me jabbing me over, and over again with cattle prods! I can't see if this is actually happening to me, but it feels like I'm being bent over backward, and slowly lifted in the air. I hear what sounds like hundreds of people moaning, groaning, and crying out in agony. I then get hit with a stench as if I'm being lowered into the bottom of a porta-potty, and submerged into what lies beneath!

Absolutely no sense of time, and I remember thinking I'm dying.

I hear this woman's voice as though she is standing right next to me speaking plain as day right into my left ear, she says, "Pray dummy pray!" To this day I still agree to disagree with my mentor as to if this was my guardian angel or her. I'll admit, it did sound like my mentor who has a strong discernment to know when someone close to her is in peril, especially with the demonic. Since I have already seen my guardian angel twice and had her save my life twice before, that's what I'm going to go with.

I am not sure how many times I recited it, but it seemed as though I recited the Our Father fifty times.

I all of a sudden am looking up at a ceiling. I can breathe, no more pain, no stench, no sounds of tortured souls, and I can move. My eyes are adjusted to the dark, and I can see I'm on my back on the bed in the master bedroom. I sit up, and it takes me a moment, but I suddenly realize I have urinated and defecated in my pants!

Two things are very significant here, one that hasn't happened to me since I was a young boy, and two something so evil reached down into my very soul, and my body just let go as if I had died? I did have a near death experience, and some close to me feel as though I did, I have always thought of it as being a survivor of an extreme demonic attack. It's not important what it was, what is important is whatever did happen that night resulted in me walking away from the field of paranormal investigations, and spiritual warfare. I was shaken to my very core. I stood up from the bed, and I had a light jacket on. I took it off, and wrapped it around my waist, as I was embarrassed. I walked out into the living room, and Anna says to me, "I was just getting ready to come looking for you, everything ok?" I said, of course, I asked how long was I back there, she replied, "Oh about thirty minutes." She commented on how quiet I was and asked what was I doing back there. I told her I was quiet because I did not want to wake your daughter up, and I just wanted to relax, and see if I could feel or sense anything.

    I apologized to her that I needed to go, that it been quiet, and I would go home and review evidence and get back to her. That was the last time we spoke. I found out weeks later through my former team member who worked with her, that after that night, things went back to normal for her and her daughter. My friend also told me the situation at work was much better too. My friend was the one who actually told Anna what happened to me because I had shared it with him. Anna e-mailed me how bad she felt about what had happened to me. I made light of it, and just replied back, "Oh, all in a day's work!"

My theory today is this; my attack was planned from the beginning of the first case. I feel as though there was more than one entity at work here, and that they were in cahoots with one another. The power of prayer my friends, the power of prayer! One last interesting fact about these cases was, everyone, involved either knew each other personally, or professionally, and everyone knew me, and it seems like it was deliberate that they were all thrown across my path, and I was the one put in a position to help, or not, them all.

I somehow managed to, for the most part, stay away from throwing myself back into the ring. As time went on I began to realize just how bad my attack had messed up my mind. For the next several months to almost a year, I was really hanging on emotionally by my fingernails. I was struggling with watching my wife battling cancer, struggling at work, struggling with referring cases that came my way out to other teams, etc. When I did council someone through their paranormal issues on the phone or by e-mail, I felt like a hypocrite because I wasn't out there practicing what

I preached. It also didn't help matters that we were still experiencing paranormal drive-bys on and off.

One such incident was especially upsetting because it involved one of my dogs. One of my Mastiffs, all of a sudden, became very ill. He wouldn't eat, was lethargic, vomiting, diarrhea, and his face swelled up as though he was having a severe allergic reaction to something. He didn't get into anything in the house like the trash, chocolate, medication prescription or otherwise. We do live in the desert, and he is an indoor/outdoor dog, so I checked him for a bee sting, spider, scorpion or snake bite. Nothing! I have worked in the animal care industry as a veterinary technician for over 20 years, so now I'm really starting to worry. I rushed him down to the clinic I was working at for one of the overnight emergency Doctors to look at him.

They did a thorough physical exam, did blood work, ran a variety of different types of tests, and all were unsuccessful in determining what was going on. I got this crazy idea and decided to leave my dog at the clinic for observation for a little while, so I could run home, and continue my search for something out of the normal. I got home and turned my dog's kennel upside down. I took his toys, blankets, water and food bowls out, and even picked up the bottom removable mat to peek underneath, and there it was.

    I wasn't positive that what I was looking at, was what I thought I was looking at, but I removed it just the same. I found what appeared to be a small piece of root about the size of my pinky finger. This root felt to the touch as though it had a hard putty, clay type texture to it. It matched nothing I had in the house or any plant, shrubbery, or trees I had outside. As I handled this root more I began to become ill. I took the root, made a small hole in the ground outside, put the root in the hole, said a couple of exorcism-deliverance prayers, poured some holy water into the hole, followed by some gasoline. I then lit the gasoline on fire and allowed the root to burn for a minute or so before filling the hole in. I poured more holy water on the ground where the hole was, said a couple more prayers, and called it a day. By the time I got inside, I felt like a brand new man, and my phone was ringing.

    I answered the phone, and it's my dog's Doctor. She says my dog has made a complete recovery, and it's like nothing ever happened to him. He's eating, drinking and bouncing off the walls, so come and get him!

    What we were dealing with is what we call a demonic calling card. They are all not the same, but they are something a demon comes by, and drops off at your home. They are designed to make anyone that comes in contact with them to become very ill. If the calling card is not found soon, those affected by them get worse and worse, and sometimes the situation can become life-threatening. They are not hidden so that without a little effort they can't be found. They want you to find them so you know they have been there, and that they are checking in on you to make sure you have not gotten lazy, and slipped up, and re-opened a door for them to re-enter your home. I'm telling you, these things can really ruin your day! They may not have a skeleton key to use on your front door, and be able to pitch a tent in your yard, because you have successfully protected both, but they continue to creep around especially if you've been touched or have engaged in battle against them.

    I was out back one day doing some cleanup duty after my dogs, and I heard an odd noise over by my pool. My pool is fenced off from the dogs. I head over to take a look around, and something shoved me into the deep end of my pool! My pool is drained! That really hurt! I decided to attach some blessed medals to all the outside water faucets. I also laid hands on my water system and prayed over it. Now

I water down with a hose my roof, and all the trees, shrubbery and bushes all around the perimeter of my yard, front, and back.

You simply cannot make this stuff up, please pray for me.

10
The Holy Spirit

So, I have essentially at this point in time, walked away from the field of paranormal investigations, and spiritual warfare other than continuing to pray to God to continue to protect my wife and I. I'm on this roller coaster ride with my wife, and her battle with cancer, and still dealing with the occasional paranormal occurrence in, and around our home. I am occasionally still taking calls from time to time from people needing advice on how to deal with their own paranormal issues. I'm trying to keep a low key profile at work too because I'm still witnessing myself, and other co-workers experiencing paranormal activity at the workplace, and everyone who has an experience comes running to you know who!

It wasn't until years later I realized that where I was working at this time, in the oncology department at an animal hospital for ten years probably wasn't the best for me for emotional health. Every patient I see is dying from cancer, my wife has cancer, there's paranormal activity all around the workplace, and I get blamed for a lot of it, and I come home, and it's a whole lot of the same! By the time I realized I had a severe case of compassion fatigue, my job released me because they had nothing in place to deal with employees with emotional issues, they just cut them loose.

One day while I was still working there, approaching my departure, but unaware of my being released, a gentleman I knew who worked at one of the pet cemeteries in town, was at the clinic picking up bodies of patients that been euthanized throughout the day, came up to me and told me of a client who had buried their dog at his cemetery was desperate for help with some extremely scary paranormal events occurring at her house, and would I please look into it for him.

I so wanted to say no, but he was a friend and used to allow me (for years) give ghost tours at his cemetery, so I reluctantly agreed. What I didn't tell him was that I was going to reach out to a pastor friend of mine, and have him handle the case.

My pastor friend was more than happy to do me this favor, and I awaited her feedback. Keep in mind that although Priests, Pastors, Ministers, and Reverends know what spiritual warfare is, most are not readily or emotionally willing to jump into it with both feet when it comes to the paranormal, or cases that might involve the demonic. A couple of days went by, and my pastor friend called me and told me something I have never had a person in that position tell me before. Now, I have had priests reach out to me after performing a house blessing where the house was discovered to be under demonic infestation, and when I show up, the priest is actually waiting for me outside the house, and doesn't have any intention of going back in the house, just to get me up to speed on what he feels is happening inside. My pastor friend tells me that she got to the house in question, and she couldn't bring herself to even knock on the door. She is willing to try, and see it through, but only if I help her.

    The first available time I had to go, my pastor friend could not be there. I was seriously considering re-scheduling, but Sharon, who was having a good day said, "Don't do that, I'll go with you!" I didn't have the best feeling going into this as it was, but I really had reservations about taking Sharon due to her condition.

    Oh well, buckle your chin straps here we go. Sharon and I arrive at the location, and I must admit, not the best part of town. Every town has their ghetto, but this was that area where those that live there dream about moving on up to the ghetto! This did feed into the fear I already had going into this. How could it not?

Sharon and I walk up to the front door, and I could totally understand why my pastor friend did not even want to knock. I can't really put my finger on it exactly what this was, but it felt like there was some kind of unseen gauntlet positioned in front of the residence pushing back, keeping us at bay. Sharon even commented under breath, "Whoa!" She looked at me and asked well, you going to knock, or do you want me to? I knocked.

Have you seen the original black and white version of The Wolfman with Lon Chaney, Sr? For those of you that have, the front door of this residence slowly opens up, and I find myself looking at Malerva, the Gypsy woman from the Wolfman! With this accent, somewhere sounding like Eastern Europe, Malerva, "Angie" was her name, invites us in. We enter into the most depressing one bedroom apartment I have ever seen or physically been in. Everything was in one room, bathroom, kitchen, master bedroom literally in one room! No kitchen counter, just the small fridge, washer & dryer unit up against one wall. A toilet up against another wall, no bathroom sink. A small mattress in the middle of the floor. I felt really bad, because I didn't know some people lived this way. I noticed there was no shower at the same time I noticed Angie was barefoot, and the bottoms of her feet were absolutely black! Angie's accent was very thick, and there was a bit of a language barrier, but I listened as she told me how she fled the old country to get away from some demons that had followed her all the way here to America.

She goes on to tell us that she has captured the demons in her luggage, and points across the room to two large leather satchels that are wrapped in chains, and padlocked shut!

Yeah, I know! As she continues telling us this fantastic tale, Sharon and I are fixated on these two pieces of luggage.

All of a sudden, Sharon and I hear what sounds like a faint cry or grunt come from inside one of the bags, and then the bag moves a little! I look over at Sharon, and she's already staring at me wide-eyed, and Angie says. "See, I told you."

So, a million things are going through my mind at that moment, and Sharon says, "This isn't good, I feel like I'm standing in a tank of soup." I too felt odd, pressure on the brain, ears popping like at an altitude.

Angie asks us to please just take the luggage with us, and get rid of it. She says, "I don't care how you do it, just do not open the bags, if you do the demons will escape, and then attach to you or come back for me." Angie tells us that just about everything she owns is in those bags, but she doesn't care, she just wants the demons gone.

Angie appears to start looking as though she might begin to get a little hysterical, so I agreed, and Sharon and I grabbed the luggage and left.

Before you judge me, no, I had no intention of throwing away all this woman's belongings. Can you guess what happened next? I just may be the only exorcist to ever perform an exorcism on luggage?! I'm not going to lie, I did have thoughts that perhaps there was a cat or small dog or God forbid Angie abducted a child, and stuck it in one of these bags.

This was a very different, and one of a kind situation that I had never encountered before. We had the luggage in our trunk of the car, and this is where they were going to stay for the time being. Sharon and I did agree that the longer we were around these bags we began to feel ill, paranoid and had a sense of something bad coming our way. I decided to take authority over the exorcism with Sharon, and my pastor friend assisting.

When I showed up at my pastor friend's home and told her our story, and asked for her help, she gave me one of the craziest looks I think anyone has ever given me, and believe me I've gotten many of them!

A big build up to a relatively uneventful ceremony of the rites. The three of us did agree that the luggage did feel much lighter to pick up than they did before. All the weird feelings we were having around the luggage had also left us. I was looking forward to surprising Angie by bringing her luggage, and her life belongings back to her. I decided to leave Sharon because she was still having her good and bad days, but I felt there was something lurking at Angie's, and I didn't want to expose her. I did say to my pastor friend, "Hey, you got me into this mess, you're coming with me." My plan was to just get in and out of there, and be done with it, and on my way. Things never go as planned, do they?. Angie was very surprised and happy to see us, and to also get her belongings back. I assured her that her luggage was demon free. Angie asked us to please come in before we left to pray with her. She said there are still demons here, and I need help sending them on their way. I learned my lesson that day to always be prepared.

I hadn't planned on this, so all I had on me was holy water. We went into the apartment, and I'm telling you, it felt absolutely as though you were in a dungeon. OK, I have never been in a dungeon, but it sure looked like one from pictures I've seen. Very, very dark, bad odors, more than that of an old woman's body odor. We stood in a circle in the middle of the room, and held hands, and began to pray.

It really felt as though we were circling the wagons, and getting ready to defend against an attack, but from what? My eyes were closed, and my head was down. It all of a sudden felt as though someone that I've known all my life came up behind me, and gently hugged me. I raised my head and leaned back as though to rest my head on someone's shoulder. I opened my eyes, and there was a figure of a person completely engulfed in flames, hovering above us. I had this overwhelming feeling of complete peace, and love like never before. I watched this beautiful apparition raise its right arm, and slowly start turning to its right circling while making the sign of the cross in all four directions of the room. As it did this, it sounded as though we were in a pig pen with a bunch of piglets running around squealing, and running out of the room. When this figure stopped back at its original position, I closed my eyes, and slowly lowered my head, I remember being hit by the smell of an open field, full of wildflowers, and I opened my eyes. The room was so bright, it was blinding as if the roof had been ripped off, and the sun was directly overhead beaming down!

There they were, Angie, and my friend, just staring at me. They didn't say a word, but clearly, they knew something had happened to me, and happened to us which was a complete game changer beyond our comprehension. I gave my holy water to Angie, and told her, "You won't be needing this, but if you do, just start flailing it at whatever bad thing it is you want gone, and it will go trust me!"

My friend and I walked about a block back to our cars, and never spoke a word. We got in our cars and went our separate ways. I got home, sat down at my kitchen table, and began sobbing like a baby. I can't tell you why just couldn't control it. I did decide at that moment to call my friend, and share my experience. My friend was actually driving on the freeway when she answered her phone. When I told her what happened, she actually pulled over on the side of the freeway, got out of her car, and started dancing.

She said to me I have been a good Christian all my life, became a Pastor, and I pray every day to see the Holy Spirit, and you're the one that has the vision. She added, "I'm so, so happy for you, and I know it's a sin, but I'm so jealous too!" She was kidding of course, about being jealous that is.

I'm not going to begin to even try and articulate, and put it into words exactly what happened to me that day. What I can say is this, it was an awakening for me. It was a clear message from God that He had my back, and to fear no more. That he put me on this earth to do exactly what I'm doing today, and he would not let the enemy harm me. Just like that, I'm back in the demon bustin' biz, for real!

When I made that announcement to Sharon, she smiled, and said, "You had never left it, you were just on a short vacation."

Not very short I thought, almost a year. I said to Sharon, "You know that's the one thing I didn't work out with God, and put in the fine print of my contract, "PAID VACATIONS!!"

11
Black Dogs And Beasts

The time has come to share with you the story I mentioned at the beginning of the introduction of this book. This is the singular incident that took me to a whole new level, one that I could never have imagined existed unless I had experienced it myself. Two extremely important things happened to me that night. Although these demonic entities, fallen angels, whichever you prefer, are the singular most vile, and disgusting creatures, and present the most lethal threat spiritually, and otherwise to the existence of mankind. I have developed a healthy respect of them in the sense that they did play by rules handed down by God when they were banished down to earth to exist side by side with us. And, because it would take something that powerful to require the power of Jesus Christ himself to keep in check. If anything sticks with you from this book, let it be this chapter, and that whenever, and God forbid it never happens to you, that you bring these creatures down on you, that you need to get down on your knees, and pray out loud to God to please in the name of his son, Jesus

Christ, to send down some of his most faithful warrior angels to escort these creatures to the foot of the cross for Jesus to deal with them. If God does that for you, then you need to change your life around, and worship him the rest of your life! If you have faith, true faith, and I pray that you do, then prepare yourself to witness through me, and through the words written on these next few pages, the absolute power of Jesus Christ. I feel the need to caution you as you read on that you just might want to have your Bible, and holy water handy. May God bless you.

I'm riding on a white cloud right now. It has been a week or so since my life-changing vision of the Holy Spirit. At the same time, Sharon seems to be having a rough week. I'm trying to be as close to her as I can, and use this renewed strength, spiritually, that I have to raise her spirits. She is strong, and she is also stubborn too.I know it's best for her at this time to concentrate on getting better, and leave the demon-busting to me. As much as I want to discuss cases with her, and take her with me to work cases, I must find a way to, for the time being, go work cases on my own for now. I have a list longer than my arm of people who want to help me on my cases, but I simply cannot bring anyone who is not trained to handle the darker cases along for the ride, simply too dangerous to do so.

One evening after Sharon had fallen asleep, I sneak off into the office in our home to check my e-mails and contact us forms off of the Ghost.B.Gone.Biz website. There are a few messages there, and for some apparent reason this one message is standing out to me. I double click on it, and I actually get a slight head rush. The message is from a woman with the last name of Burke. She tells me that a week before sending me this message is when she experienced something very odd one day. She is a single Mother, with two young boys, one ten and one fifteen. The three moved out to Las Vegas several months back, from Los Angeles. They are originally from New Orleans. Her sons are both in school, and doing well, and she says that they are really good boys. Every Mother says that right?! I do believe her though. Even though this is just an e-mail, I get a good vibe from it. Sometimes you just have to lower your guard and go with your gut, and as I said before, I'm riding high on this renewed spirituality, and love for God, and I'll be honest, I feel a little indestructible. She goes on to describe that one afternoon after school, her younger son, as he usually does, stops at the small playground in their gated community to play before coming home.

On this particular day, her younger son comes running in the house as if something or someone is chasing him. She said that he appeared frightened, and had a hard time catching his breath.

After he calmed down, he told her that this weird little kid, a boy, came up to him at the park, and wanted to play with him. This odd little boy wanted Mrs. Burke's son to go somewhere with him to show him something. Mrs. Burke said that her son told the boy no, and the boy got upset. The odd boy began to scare Mrs. Burke's son, so he ran over to some of his other friends on the other side of the park. The young Burke asked his friends if any of them knew that little boy, and their response was, "What boy?"

He pointed at the other boy, and said "That kid there." These other friends of his saw no other boy. He insisted, "That kid right there" and pointed. Same response, no one could see this odd little boy. The young Burke told his Mom that he got really mad at the other kids because they were trying to play a trick on him, so he left and headed home. He told her that this little boy started to follow him home. The faster he walked the faster the other little boy walked. Mrs. Burke commented that her son ended up running home with this odd little boy in hot pursuit. Mrs. Burke said that her son made a very odd statement that sent chills down her spine.

Her son said that the little boy ran like a dog, down on his hands!! Mrs. Burke ran outside and looked everywhere for this little boy, and he was nowhere to be found. She knew, as every Mother would know, that her son wasn't lying, and was genuinely scared.

What she wasn't sure of was if her son was having some kind of episode. Mental episode that is!!

The family all ate dinner together that night, watched a little T.V., and she helped her older son with his homework, and before she knew it, it was bedtime. She tucked them in, stayed up a little longer, and then retired for the evening.

Mrs. Burke was awakened up in the middle of the night because she could feel her younger son crawl into bed with her. Not unusual, he did that often. She also knew he had quite an ordeal earlier, and expected it on this evening. After a few moments, Mrs. Burke realized how cold it had gotten in the room, and it felt as though she was lying next to a block of ice. She then smelled a really bad odor and thought maybe her son had an accident in the bed from being so upset, and frightened earlier. She tried to turn the lamp on that was on her nightstand, but it didn't work. She got up, walked over to the bathroom, turned on the bathroom light, and turned around.

There was no one in her bed! She admitted to me that now she was truly freaked out, and her mind was blown. She went to check on her boys, and they were fast asleep. She was a little too freaked out to go back to bed, so she fell asleep in a chair in the living room. When she saw her son the next morning, even though she already knew the answer, she just had to ask him if he crawled into bed with her the night before.

Without any hesitation, and without skipping a beat, her son says, "No Mommy, it was the little boy!" She dropped her coffee cup sending it crashing to the floor. She felt dizzy and sat down at the kitchen table.

She asked her son, "Baby don't play with me, what are you saying?"

Her son tells her that he got up in the middle of the night to get a snack. While he was in the kitchen, there was a knock on the back door, and it was the little boy. He said that the little boy seemed fine, but he said he needed help, and to please let him in, so he did. Well, to say she got extremely angry with her son would be an understatement. She turned her house upside down, and could not find the boy. She didn't want to find the boy, but the alternative was even worse, to think he might not be a real flesh and blood kid. She confessed to me that she was of Creole descent, and grew up around a lot of crazy, crazy stuff.

I asked her like what, and she said, "Like voodoo, hoodoo, witchcraft, you name it."

I asked her, "So you're a witch."

She said, "Hell no, but my whole family was involved in that, and that's why as soon as I met someone like the boy's Father, who could take me away from that, and to somewhere like L.A., I jumped at it!"

I asked her where the boy's Father was, and she said, "dead."

I told her that I'm sorry, but I have to ask, "How did he die?"

She said, "In his sleep from a heart attack".

I told her all about Sharon and asked her if there was more to the story of his death.

She said, "Now that you mention it, he did for quite some time have night terrors that an old hag would come to him in his dreams, and hold him down, and have sex with him."

I kept my mouth shut, because I didn't want to add fuel to the fire and add to the hysteria. I suspected a trans-generational curse of some kind passed down through her ancestry, and onto her. I told her to try, and keep it together, keep her kids close, and stay strong until I could get there, which might be a few days away. I want you, the reader, to understand that sometimes, depending on just what you're dealing with, things can escalate very fast. It doesn't always start with a Ouija board, a bed shaking, trips to the Doctors, and Psychiatrists, then someone strapped to a bed throwing up green pea soup all over the room. A curse means there was a conjuring, and a deal was made, and they are part of the deal.

Although the power of Christ compels them, they are older than time, all knowing, and very powerful. They can pretty much do whatever they want if they feel they were invited, and have permission to be there, and they are there for the long haul until something more powerful, and holy comes along to send them on their way.

A couple of days later, it's late in the evening, and my phone is ringing off the hook. I answer the phone, and it's Mrs. Burke.

She's hysterical. She says that over the past couple of days her youngest son changed into someone or something, and she didn't even recognize him anymore. He attacked his older brother, and the attack was severe enough for her to send him away to stay with some friends for a little while. She is begging me to come now.

She said that her son is barricaded in his room, and she can't get to him. Sharon is asleep, and I made the decision to go. I grabbed my travel bag that has everything I think I might need, and I leave Sharon a note, and I leave.

I pull up to the house, and I see a woman sitting out on the curb with just a robe on. As I slowly pull up, she stands up and walks back into her yard, and just stands there staring at me.

I get out of my car, and as I walk up to her she says to me, "Rev. Shawn…"

I shook my head yes. I start to say, not sure what, but she side cuts me off, and says, "That thing upstairs is not my son, what have they done to my baby?" She begins to cry and abruptly sits right down on the stairs to the front door. I don't say another word and walked inside. The feeling inside the home hit me right in the face like a right cross. It stopped me dead in my tracks, because I have experienced this feeling before, and my mind or inner voice, if you will, was screaming at me not to go any further.

    I took one step back, got down on my knees just outside the front door, and began to pray. I said the Our Father, the Hail Mary, the prayer to St. Michael, (short version in English), and pulled the St. Jude card out of my front shirt pocket, and recited that including asking St. Jude out loud to petition on my behalf to ask Jesus to please send down help to me of any kind so that I may not have to walk this path alone. I then crawled on my hands and knees over the threshold to exhibit extreme humility!

    Once in the house, I get to my feet and make my way upstairs toward her son's bedroom. I'm not sure which room it is, but I was pretty sure I would figure it out. I got to the top of the stairs, and the first room I see, the door is shut, and I can see the light from inside the room under the door flickering. I call out to her son and get no response. I call out again, again no response. I turn the doorknob, and the door just opens slightly, but there is something big, and heavy wedged up against it. I can see into the room, and I see what appears to be a small boy sitting on the floor on the other side of the room. I call out again, nothing. I decided to really put my shoulder, and legs into it, and try to push the door open. I push, and push, and push, and finally there just enough of an opening for me to squeeze through. Once in the room, I realize that there were bunk beds wedged up behind the door. I slowly start to walk over to her son, and it sounds as though there is something circling me snapping its fingers in my ears. Her son looks up at me, and I'm staring at an old man. I mean an old man, like in his 80's – 90's perhaps. Is this Grandpa Burke I thought?

I somehow all of a sudden realize I'm staring at Mrs. Burke's son, and then I'm hit with the same face I was hit with when I was last attacked! This time I'm able to drop to my knees, and I'm completely limp like I have no bones, I'm all folded over on myself. I know I'm looking down and must have had my eyes closed because I can't see anything. I'm in some discomfort, but nothing like before. I open my eyes slowly, and the room is dark. The flickering light has completely gone out. There's just enough moonlight, and reflection of street light coming through a window I can make out shapes, but that's about it.

I look down and then realize there's an unusual glow entering about the room, then bam, I'm in a full on vision of the past, and I'm a young, very young boy back in Colts Neck, N.J., and I'm running home being chased by three big kids that were much older, and much bigger than me, they were the neighborhood bullies, and I was scared to death of them.

They are gaining on me, and I'm convinced I'm about to get caught and then beaten to death by these guys. I run out into the street, and right in front of an oncoming car that has to slam on its brakes, and lay on the horn at me as I fall down.

I look up, and getting out of the car is my Dad! Now, what my Father proceeded to do to these three bullies, today, would probably land him in jail, but I'll never forget that feeling like you're about to die, and then you realize you're saved!! My vision turns into me on my knees, and I'm in the desert. This feels different though, this is no vision, this is real. I'm in the desert, and the thought enters my mind that maybe I got mugged and dumped in the desert or maybe I had a stroke and ended up walking out in the desert?!

Wait a minute, there's that 90-year-old man still sitting on the ground in front of me, just a few feet away. At this point, the level of confusion is off the charts, but I'm also enjoying a sense of real comfort, and peace. This unusual glow in this landscape became a little brighter like a sunset, and sunrise at the same time, if that's possible. I notice a shadow coming over me from my right, and extending out in front of me on the ground several feet. I glance over, and I'm looking at Jesus hanging on the cross!

My eyes are frozen on this vision. My Father and Savior are here!! Am I dead? Am I on Calvary?? Am I in Heaven??? I absolutely cannot take my eyes off of my Savior. Throw everything you have ever seen or imagined about the crucifixion out the window. I know I'm looking at Jesus, but he simply looks like a bloody, beaten, disfigured, and mangled slab of meat hanging on a tree. A sight that I should find horrifying, and yet to me it is the most beautiful thing I have ever laid my eyes on. I'm drawn to it like a moth to a flame. I begin to crawl on my hands and knees toward the cross. It's real alright, and am still wondering if I'm dead, and in Heaven.

Stronger than at any other point in my life since my Father (may he R.I.P.), has passed, that I feel him walk up behind me, put his hand gently under my armpits, and gently start lifting me up, and onto my feet. As I raise up and begin to stand, I reach out and hold on to the cross, and hand over hand as if climbing a rope, I also use the cross to help me get to my feet. I'm standing now, and almost to Christ. I get on my tippy toes, and stretch my neck forward, and upward, and kiss Jesus on his left foot. To this day I can still remember tasting the dirt, mud, fresh and dried blood, from Jesus' foot. I also will never forget that Jesus left foot was placed over his right. That's always the first thing I look at now when I see a crucifix. I'm often asked for as much detail as I can remember about this vision. The cross appeared to look more like a tree than a cross, a traditional one that is, and I did not actually see nails, but I did see something tying him to the tree in several parts of his body, ankles, thighs, hips, armpits, elbows, and wrists! No clothing whatsoever!! His head was positioned in a downward position, and there was something on his head like a crown, for lack of a better word, but I could not make out if this was thorns.

At this very moment, without anyone saying anything or needing any further direction, I know exactly what needs to be done. I turn around and look at this old man. He looks up at me, and I know that old man is, in fact, the little boy, the young Burke. I walk over to him, and as I walk up on him I can see he is sitting on a path. The path goes down a hill, and at the bottom of this hill are several cloaked figures, and several black dogs. I cannot make out any features on the figures, female, male demons, or phantoms. The dogs are quite frightening. They look like a cross between a hyena, and a black German Shepherd. They are very low in the rear end. A couple of them were scooting on their rear ends as if to scratch an itch, or perhaps that was how they defecate because they would leave a trail of some sort of dark gooey substance like dark bloody diarrhea. I kneel down in front of the young boy and begin to pray. As I pray I am pouring holy water on his head. I pull out my anointing oil and anoint his forehead. I take out my blessed salts and sprinkle some on his head, and as best I can on the ground around him. I take out a piece of blessed raw Frankincense in crystal form, I raise the boy's head up, and force a piece into his mouth. I take out a book of some deliverance prayers, and while touching him with my left hand I begin to pray away! I can't be positive, or exact on how much time passed. I prayed on until the little boy looked up at me, and he no longer appeared as an old man, but an innocent child of God.

At that moment we were back in his bedroom. The light was back on, and an overwhelming sense of calm to what was first raging storm when I first arrived. The boy and I touched foreheads, and we began to cry. No words were spoken. We got up, made our way downstairs, and there was his Mother. He ran into her arms, and they hugged and continued to cry. I sat down at the kitchen table to relax, gather my thoughts, and reflect on what had just happened. Mrs. Burke looked at me, and I could see it in her eyes, she knew something miraculous had happened, but exactly what she wasn't sure. The only thing I could think to say was, "I'm hungry, how about we order some pizza?!" We all had one of those break the ice, release the tension laughs. They sat down, I called a pizza parlor on the corner, we waited for the delivery, and I treated! We ate, and never spoke a word of what happened.

As I left, Mrs. Burke gave me one of those hugs that is almost painful, and breathtaking, and looked at me, and said, "I made arrangements to move back to L.A. to be with family, we're leaving right away."

I said, "God be with you sister". We have spoken from time to time since that night. I'm happy to report she, and her family are doing well. Transgenerational curses, we don't know a lot about them.

I have an old saying about them though, "You can't live with them, and you can't go back to when the deal was done, and change it, but it's nothing that your faith in the power of Jesus Christ can't handle".

In doing research on my own ancestry for this book, I discovered Whittingtons back in England during the witch hunts, and trials that took active roles, and perhaps that's the reason also for a lot of the paranormal drive-bys that still occur at my house.

A witch will tell you, oh by the way I can take care of that for you. I'm not going to do any witch bashing here, I do have some friends that are witches, but for now, I'll just keep doing that thing that I do!!!

12

Paranormal Ministry

As I'm writing this, I am getting ready to celebrate three years on the air with my online paranormal radio show, Vegas Supernatural. Kind of a big deal considering it was my wife's idea, and I have no idea what I'm doing. According to the station manager, my show is doing well, and I have a lot of listeners, and my listener base is growing all the time. My wife also loves the show and considering she is my producer and pays for my air time, I'll just continue to not have a clue what I'm doing until further notice, it seems to be working for me at the moment. If you go for that sort of thing, the show airs live, Monday nights online.

I'm also proud to announce that I also teach two college courses for a Bible college and theological seminary. Introduction to Spiritual Warfare, and Introduction to Paranormal Ministry. If you feel the calling to this ministry, you can contact me by filling out the contact form on our website, www.ghost-b-gone.biz.

Why paranormal ministry, many people first reach out to their priest, pastor, minister, what have you, and more and more I'm helping people who have been turned away from their church when they went there for help. I'm hoping not only to reach out to those who have a calling but to clergy that might be interested in knowing a little more about the paranormal world.

I thought along the lines of paranormal ministry, I would share several cases with you that have always stood out to me as cases that are extremely unique, and yet challenging to both the deliverance minister and the paranormal investigator.

***

"The case of Martin & Gail" – since I did make mention in the previous chapter of the black dogs, I thought I would start with where I first encountered them. (Martin & Gail) were a retired elderly couple, married, and appeared happy.

They, of course, struggled with the usual issue of being on a fixed income and trying to make a go out of a home-based business. In addition to their paranormal issues, I suspect there was more underneath. All you can do is ask the tough questions, and hope they are honest with you. According to my clients, the house they were in was the odd house in the neighborhood. There was a history of tenants not staying more than a few months at a time, and just breaking their lease, and leaving. For this reason, they got a deal on rent. I tried to talk to neighbors, and the landlord and everyone was tight-lipped. They claimed the house was swallowing up their money, literally. Money was just disappearing.

Their dog, a cocker spaniel, came down with an extreme infestation of ticks and fleas. The bug guy had been there a few times to spray, but the infestation would return. They couldn't figure out where the bugs were coming from. This is very odd because Las Vegas does not have fleas and ticks.

Gail started finding a black tarry substance in her bed She first thought Martin was having accidents in their bed. He claimed it wasn't him. She went on to describe how they were changing and becoming people they weren't. They were starting to fight all the time, and their health was rapidly declining.

One morning Gail woke up, and a very odd feeling that something was very wrong. She called out to Martin a couple of times, and he didn't answer or move. She feared the worst, and pulled the covers off of him. To her utter shock, it was not Martin next to her, it was a big black dog! She screamed, and jumped back while this dog crawled out of the bed, onto the floor, and through the wall. Martin then came in because he heard her scream. She told him the story, and if it wasn't for the black tarry substance left behind in the bed, he wouldn't have believed her.

They both agreed to contact me. Martin did later that same day. He found his cocker spaniel cowering under an end table in the living room, and it wouldn't come out. He did actually see the black dog in the hallway leading to the bedroom and saw it defecate that black substance they had been seeing before it vanished through a closed door.

On my first time there, I was coming down a ladder after looking into the crawl space above. As I came down the ladder something tapped me on my shoulder, I ignored it. When I was on the floor, Gail said, "Did you see that?"

I said, "What did you see?" She pointed at a coin on the floor. She said that it appeared right out of the ceiling, fell, and hit me on my shoulder.

She then said, "See I told you the house was taking our money!"

In the next couple of days, they found their dog dead on the back porch. Something had attacked it. Animal Control claimed it had to be a big hungry coyote that got in the yard. Perhaps, but we knew better.

I decided that what Sharon and I needed to do was to give them hope, and strength in the form of knowing we wanted to help. My wife got Gail a job, and I talked the Martin's into going to see a psychiatrist. I could tell he needed to bare his soul to someone, because he had a lot of bottled up, and he would get more help from a licensed physician for that. I got them both to start going back to church weekly for confession, mass, and communion.

I performed a thorough cleansing, and blessing of the property, and home, and bought them a little time. But, ultimately they had to join the list of tenants to break their lease and leave early. This case would end up being classified as unresolved but closed.

***

"Pet Cemetery" – a local pet cemetery here in town is a favorite location of mine. Sharon and I used to give ghost tours there. Yes, the location is very haunted. The former owner of the cemetery lived in a house next door to the cemetery most of her adult life until she passed away in that home, but she never left. The pet cemetery was once a human cemetery and I had come face to face with many of them over the years. If you had pets buried there and it was in your will to be buried with your pets that could be arranged. Such was the case with a local Vegas who took part in a murder-suicide. Shortly after the burial, a series of poltergeist type paranormal activity took over the grounds. We also got word that the house by the cemetery was sold off with that piece of land, and was scheduled to be torn down. I knew I had to get in there, and speak to the spirit of the former cemetery owner, and explain to her why she had to leave. I was also aware of her love for the cemetery, so I planned to use that to my advantage, and to solicit her help. I got in there one night, yes I trespassed; keep that under your hat. I spoke openly and honestly to her and explained to her that her house was being torn down and that we had a trouble maker ghost at the cemetery. I convinced her, at least I believe so, that her place was over there with her pets, friends, and family. That way she could keep an eye on things, and get the trouble maker to settle down. I put a large bouquet of flowers down on the foot of the fireplace. I told her the flowers were for her, and to take them with her.

At that moment we heard what sounded like someone heading our way from the master bedroom. We witnessed a bright self-illuminating orb about the size of a softball float down the hallway, and across the living room. This orb headed straight for the fireplace and hovered over the flowers for a moment or two before floating straight up the chimney. I was pleased to have captured her orb in a still shot before she was gone.

It wasn't long after that, the home was torn down, and a bank was built on that location. Things quickly calmed down over at the cemetery, and to this day, the former owner is often seen walking a couple of her pets (spirit pets), around the perimeter of the grounds keeping an eye on things.

She is also occasionally seen tending to the garden there. I did one day pop into that bank and asked to speak to the manager. I asked him straight up if he, or any of his employees, or even clients had experienced any paranormal activity in the bank. He looked at me wide-eyed, and froze! I smiled, handed him my card, and walked out.

I'm still waiting for that call...

***

"Haunted Old Vegas" – Sharon and I were asked to look into an apparent haunting at a beautiful old home in town that had become very difficult to sell, because of spirit activity in and around the home.

If the spirits there didn't like the potential buyers, they weren't having it! I could write another book on just this location, but I'll give the abridged version here. Two deaths tied to the home that we know of. Both were the former owners.

The home then went through a period where it was believed to have been used by organized crime figures. All in all Sharon and I made contact with the spirit of the former female matriarch of the home, and she became a friend with Sharon. The spirit would psychically share things with Sharon that no one knew about the home, and some of the things that happened there, sometimes even following Sharon to continue the discussion there.

We were finally able to ascertain that there were at least five human spirits being held there by one malevolent, perhaps demonic entity, or non-human entity born from the violence that had occurred there during the bad years. I have one still photo of the female spirit in mention here in the reflection of a mirror, and one still photo of the malevolent entity in the form of a black mass at the top of a staircase hiding under a landing. This thing did not want you using the stairs, and you better be holding onto the railings tight, because it very often would try to push or throw you down the stairs! The home and the surrounding land/yard were massive. Therefore, we had to make many trips to bless one specific area at a time. We did our best and were finally able to get the ugly "Mr.Not So Nice," as he became to be known as, to move on along with several of the other trapped spirits. The spirit of the female matriarch explained to Sharon she wasn't going anywhere until she found a suitable buyer!

The last we heard, the house was finally sold. I guess it all worked out. Sharon has not seen this spirit since.

***

"Ghost Town Ghost Hunting" – There's a famous little ghost town just outside of Vegas that I have frequented often. Why the spirits there are so friendly and welcoming if they like you, and you show them, and the town respect. I learned a long time ago though, that every location you find infested with spirit, you're going to find, or should I say something not so nice will find you if you're at the wrong place at the wrong time, and do say the wrong thing. These troublesome spirits are always lurking and watching. It had been a while since my wife and I had gone out ghost hunting. Ghost hunting, I never liked that term. Ghosts don't like to be hunted, would you? I prefer ghost busting, or just paranormal investigating. It had been a while since we did anything paranormal related that was fun like a haunted tour, we had just been working one dark case after another.

So, for my wedding anniversary, I decided to book a private haunted tour, and haunted investigation of the ghost town, and one of its buildings. I know, I'm quite the catch aren't I? On this night it was just Sharon and me, and the para team of the town, and a couple of guests they invited. I also knew going in that one of these guests thought she had an attachment that latched onto her from this location and wanted my help.

I made no promises, but I did keep my eye on her. The first part of the tour was over, and we began our investigation. I must admit, the whole vibe of the evening took a turn when the investigation started.

One of the investigators asked the spirits if they knew who the special guest in attendance was.

Clear as day the answer came over the ghost box, "The Rev."

Right after that, another entity there made its presence known, and also made it clear it did not want me there. It then targeted the guest in question who was already very familiar with this spirit. We were beginning to lose her, and everyone present was starting to become very uncomfortable to say the least. I got up, laid hands on this girl, and asked everyone to join me in prayer.

I clearly spoke out loud and asked for some of the friendly spirits there that had been there for a very long time, that were also very protective of this location to please join us in our effort to get the invading spirit off of this girl, and push it away from the location. AND you know what? It worked. Things calmed down right away, and it felt so light and comforting in there all of a sudden. See, it is possible to form a circle of prayer warriors of ghosts if it's for a common cause. I was so appreciative of their help, I continued my blessing of this whole location, and the surrounding area just outside. I'm happy to announce that things returned to normal, normal for the ghost town that is, but unfortunately, the girl still had this attachment, and became a client of mine.

Over a relatively short period of time, things got really bad for this girl. I actually baptized her on the side of Las Vegas Blvd in the middle of the afternoon with traffic going by, and many people pointing and staring! When the situation had almost peaked, and I feared the possession was a real possibility, I had her meet me at a Catholic church in the parking lot so we could be on hallowed ground. It is mid-day, summer in Vegas, hot, and I'm sitting in my van with her about to baptize her again. In mid-sentence, while she's talking to me, she falls asleep as if she was narcoleptic or something. Two seconds later, it becomes like a meat locker in my van. She starts to breathe heavy, and the breath coming out of her mouth was rancid.

She slowly raises her head, opens her eyes, and her eyes are completely solid black, no white of the eyes showing at all. It doesn't matter how many times you see this, every time is still shocking. She didn't say a word, she just kept staring at me. I asked, "Who are you?"

It replied, "Not known to you," a brief pause, and "You are known," it says.

I then asked it, "What do you want from this child of God?" Its whole expression changed when I asked that.

For just a second I thought it was going to lash out at me. It then says one word, "Death." Its eyes close, she lowers her head, and just as quick as it came, it was gone, and she woke up, and just continued talking to me as though nothing had happened.

I'm done, I thought, and took her by the hand, and walked her into the church to speak with my Priest. They spoke in private for a while, while I waited outside. When she finally came out, we only said a few words to one another and had to run, she was late for work.

That was the last time we saw one another. Here is the interesting and upsetting thing about all this. She was an exotic dancer and party hostess. She was unwilling to change her lifestyle, and since she was raised with no religious belief system in place, she couldn't get on board with what I was trying to do to help her. I lost her to a local witch in Vegas who took her under her wing, and filled her head with a lot of different ideas than mine and taught her rituals among other things, and I continue to pray for her today. These things happen. It is what it is.

***

"The Spirits are Watching" – I love this story. It's nice to know I have friends on the other side. Was there ever a doubt?!! There's a happy ending to the ghost town incident. A couple of weeks after Sharon and I were there, I'm sound asleep in the middle of the night, for some reason I wake up out of a dead sleep, and as I'm laying in bed I can see down my hallway, and I notice Sharon standing in the dark at the end of the hallway.

I'm fixated on her, because she is absolutely still, and I can't tell if she is okay if she's staring back at me disoriented in the dark or what? I decide to get up and go see if she needs some help. As I begin to sit up in bed, I slightly lean back, and I brush up against Sharon who is sound asleep behind me in bed! That's not Sharon at the end of the hall! Okay, so I cannot explain why, but I know now, this is not an intruder, because my two Mastiffs would already have brought me this person's lifeless body. I am also not getting the usual warning signals I feel when confronted by something with bad intentions.

Here I go, I'm up and headed down the hallway to greet my guest. I get about halfway down the hall, and I start receiving snapshots psychically of this spirit. She is a Native American spirit of a woman who was born, raised, lived, and died in this now ghost town. She expressed to me how happy she was that I had blessed some of the land out there in her town. She also explained that she along with several other spirits there, were the ones that assisted me in confronting, and moving on the angry, unclean entity present that night of the investigation. She wanted me to return the favor, and come back out to the ghost town, and bless some more of the land, and its locations there. You tell me, how could I refuse such a gracious, and heartfelt request from this beautiful energy? I told her, "Yes!"

I had to smile, and chuckle a little when the next word I received from her was, "Promise?" I promised and spent weeks trying to get back there. That day did finally come one weekend, and Sharon, a friend of ours, and I took a nice drive out there to spend the day.

I started at the town cemetery, which is the first location you come to when entering the town. I blessed and recited some of the rites at half dozen or so locations around the town that I felt were active and restless with something not good brewing. At one of these locations, I felt as though I perhaps was at the area where this Indian woman lived, because I had an overwhelming sense of welcoming, and a photo was taken of me at that moment, and it appears as though I was being photo-bombed by a spirit.

Shortly after we got home, we did see the spirit of a young boy around the house. He was harmless, and I found out from a gifted psychic that I trust that this boy also lived at one time out at the now ghost town, and he really likes me, so he came home with us. I felt bad for him and did not want to kick him out.

I knew that eventually, he would return home. Not all, but some of the spirits that follow us home from time to time from cases, aren't all negative.

If they can co-exist with Sharon and me, and some of the other family spirits here in visitation, then it's "all is well that ends or dies well!"

***

"Psychological Attack" – what makes the psychological attack even more devastating than the physical attack, is you eventually physically heal from one, where the other leaves unseen wounds that cut deep into your psyche, and the scars never go away.

These attacks change you. There is one home here in Vegas that those of us in the know in the paranormal community refer to as the Vegas horror.

This house was another one of those alleged mob hit homes. Over the period of many years, many families moved in, and then out again rather quickly, never staying in the home very long. Eventually, stories surfaced about all the very aggressive paranormal activities of this haunting that occurred to these families. So odd to have this home smack dab in a neighborhood with famous neighbors all around.

It was during renovations of the home that my one family discovered a hidden utility room behind some walls that had a washbasin and a large drainage system. It was believed murdered victims of mob hits there were chopped up and disposed of in this room. As if things weren't already bad enough, once this room was discovered, the paranormal activity became off the chart!

Then the house laid vacant for many years. The current owner at that time couldn't sell it, and moving in was out of the question. Now perhaps it was because Sharon's health was compromised because of her cancer, but when we were called in to do a cleansing, Sharon became very ill, and that's not like her. That alone threw up a red flag. We had decided ahead of time this would be as much of an in-and-out visit as possible, while still trying to accomplish as thorough a house blessing as we could.

During our first visit there we experienced what sounded like old jazz being played on an old AM radio. At times we were hit by frigid blasts of air, and then waves of putrid smells. There were times when it sounded like groups of people, men, and women, walking around with us holding full on conversations as if they were still alive, and right there with us. Eventually, we had done what we came to do, and we left. You know me, the wheels are always turning. I knew several other local teams had investigated the house, but no real progress to bring closure to this haunting had occurred. Don't ask me why, but I came up with the brilliant idea to have the owner reach out to four or five other teams that had not been there yet, and just request the founder, or just the lead investigators from each team to come, and assist in taking this location on as a joint paranormal community effort. Not always, but usually the founder or lead investigators of every team is usually the most seasoned, and experienced. I threw my hat into the ring also.

The idea was well received, and the owner began making calls. Easier said than done. It took quite some doing to get us all together, schedules and all. The day finally arrived, and it was four other investigators from four different teams, and myself.

I'll never forget, when I arrived I was the last one to get there, and everyone was outside waiting for me, including the owner. I walked up wearing my Dan Aykroyd autographed ghost-busters t-shirt, and boy o' boy did they make fun of me! I thought to myself, hey what's this, I thought we were all ghostbusters? Doesn't everyone love Dan Aykroyd? This hazing went on for a little bit, and I came to the realization that perhaps it was a way for them to relieve nervous tension. The owner closed, and locked the front door behind us, and said he would return in the morning. It was almost sunset, and we were in for the night. This is another of those stories I could write a book on, so once again you're getting the abridged version. All the usual types of personal experiences took place, and to all of our disappointment nothing earth-shattering.

At midnight or somewhere thereabouts, the psychological attacks began. No one will ever know if the order of things was decided ahead of time on the other side, but it took turns one by one passing from one investigator to another.

I can't speak for anyone else, I have no idea what exactly happened to each of the other investigators, but it snowballed after the first one decided, I'm outta' here! He actually had to break a window to leave.

Over the next couple of hours, one by one each of the other three investigators exited the premises through the same window, leaving me all alone, as far as anyone else alive being with me. I have to be honest, I was quite proud of myself for outlasting the others, and had every intention of staying until sunup. I would soon come to regret that decision. I did see what appeared to be legs from just the knees down walking through the house. I smelled and saw cigar smoke, and this cigar smoke seemed to take on the shape of a person then vanish.

I saw what appeared to be a black oozing putty type substance leak out through a wall as though the wall was a sponge, then this too vanished. I'm tired, it's late, I'm alone, and freaked out, and there is no electricity in this house, and all I have is a small battery powered camping lantern, and a flashlight. Could I have imagined all this? Absolutely!

Then I am absolutely frozen to where I sit because I notice there are two people sitting just feet from me sitting on the bottom brick ledge of a fireplace. I can't move, I can't even reach for my flashlight. There is a small amount of light emanating from the small camping lantern, and I continue staring at the two figures in the dark. My eyes begin to slightly adjust to the dark, and my night vision begins to come into focus.

I'm going to finish this chapter because this book is almost to its end, but understand that this will be the toughest experience I have ever shared or put to paper.

I realize that I'm staring at my Mother and Father! They are expressionless with no emotion, and they do not utter a word. I am being fed psychically words, and snapshots of my life. It is as though I'm slowly dying and being shown my whole life, except only the very worst moments, and me at the lowest points in my life. These apparitions of my parents are telling me what a wasted life I've had, and what a worthless example of a son, and human being I've been, and have become.

The complete feeling of loneliness and despair are beyond words. It is as though I'm slowly sinking into a dark pit, and I'm going to die all alone. I'm shown things that I have buried, and forgotten about, that I am so ashamed of that now I just wanted death to come quick!

It doesn't come, instead, I hear a voice say, "Dude, you okay?" I open my eyes, and once again I'm on my back, on the floor, looking up at the owner of the home who is standing over me, and putting his hand out to help me up. Its morning, light is coming through the windows, and I know that I have lost, and can't account for, three hours of lost time. I must have just fallen asleep, and had a nightmare, right?

You know over the years, one by one by sheer coincidence, I have run into these other investigators around town who were there that night.

Not one of them, not a single one of them, is willing to talk about that night!

***

I learned a long time ago that now I ask for the help from whatever or whoever is around me that's of love, and light to protect me, my wife, my home, and my dogs. There are a lot of spirits in visitation in my home that mean me or my family no harm. If they're going to be here, might as well put them to work. They did help out not too long ago.

Sharon and I were called out to investigate a historic site out in the middle of nowhere for real! Not open to the public, so no tourist traffic, and nearest town about a two-hour drive away. Groundskeepers there had experienced some pretty scary stuff. While I was there I was at the top of a ladder looking into a loft and felt a presence behind me, so I turned, and took a photo down the ladder. If this photo is legitimate, it has to be one of the best, if not the best ghost photo in the world. There appears to be a small girl or boy standing at the bottom of the ladder, looking up at me. I showed everyone present that day, and no one saw any kids around, nor would there be any reason for there to be.

It is interesting to me that energy can also attach itself to a photo. The night I posted and showed that photo online, Sharon walked past my office several times, and saw me sitting at my desk working away. One time she walked by the office, saw me, and went straight into the master bathroom, only to find the real me, sitting on the toilet in the bathroom! I know, TMI.

She said to me, "You're sitting at your desk right now." Before I could respond, she said to wait a minute and walked away for a few minutes.

When she came back to the bathroom, she said, "You know that kid in the photo you just posted, I just saw it walk out of your office, down the hallway, and out the back door!"

I knew then that whatever was released by me posting that could not stay in the home. Help from beyond my friends.

We still do not know exactly what the ancient pure evil entities like a Jinn or ones attached to a Dybbuk box are capable of. They had no fear of God when they were alive, and take that with them to the other side. Not that if you walk in the Christ light, that you can't bring the Holy Trinity down to rain on their parade, it's just that how much death and destruction can they dish out to you, and your loved ones before help arrives. Keep your eyes open for odd symbols written on the walls in closets, and in the garage of infested homes. Draw them down or take a picture, and do your homework. They are usually satanic in nature, which will alert you that someone in the home brought this upon them.

      Beware of attention seekers, and know when to say when, and which clients you need to cut loose. To date, I have assisted in two exorcisms and took authority over one exorcism. I wake up every morning and pray that I never, ever have to take part in the performance of the rites ever again. Not because I'm afraid, but because every time one of these battles takes place, everyone involved dies a little inside.

      As glorious as it is to bring back one of God's children from the stranglehold of one of these beasts, there are still casualties as with any battles. We all know who wins the war, the war has already been won, but there will still be many battles. If you find yourself in one of these battles, whether you are a P.O.W. or a soldier still in the fight, get help immediately. You cannot fight this fight alone. I'm always being told, I'm not religious, I'm spiritual. Or,

I'm an atheist. I can't tell you how many atheists have come to me for help, who now believe in something.

I tell everyone this, I don't judge, but whatever you do, find some higher power of love, and light that you can embrace, and pray to for inner peace and strength. Most of my clients today are ghost hunters who were at the wrong place at the wrong time, and said, and did the wrong thing, and BAM, say "Hello to your new friends..." Be careful out there brothers, and sisters!

The Final Chapter
Exorcism by Distance
Part I

Just a title, no number. I felt odd numbering this last chapter being as though it comes after Chapter 12, and due to the subject matter. I'm no different than any of you, and I'm a sinner too. I have made many, many mistakes in my life, both in and out of the paranormal field. There are though, many things that I am proud of in many respects of my life, but the most rewarding part of this spiritual roller coaster I've been on for many years is helping one of God's children in their battle of a spiritual warfare nature.

Since my first encounter with the diabolic, and first meeting those who helped me then, and since getting on the path to become ordained, I have met, and become friends with many, many truly blessed and gifted exorcists all over the world. There's an old saying, "In God's time if it's God's will." And, as God would have it, after a period of time, a large number of us have formed what I like to refer to as the special forces of spiritual warfare soldiers for God.

We are all over the world, and we are on the front lines, in the trenches, and many behind enemy lines, literally! Some of us have infiltrated some of the most dangerous cults in the world today.

What we do best and most often is send demons to the foot of the cross for Jesus to deal with.

We call it exorcism by distance. For the most severe cases of demonic activity, there is an assessment team assembled to do all the groundwork necessary in determining the severity and level of the presence of the diabolic. Once all the evidence is gathered, a council meeting determines if an exorcism is the correct next move. If it is determined an exorcism is in order, a small team nearest that location is assembled.

These small teams consist of one exorcist to take authority of the ritual, two assistants who can also take over during the rites if need be, but they are there to give the appropriate responses during the rites, and to restrain if need be, the afflicted individual. We use a woman for a woman and a man for a man. One or two prayer warriors present to just do that – pray! One camera person to document the event.

When the location, day, and time of the exorcism is decided, word is sent out all throughout the entire exorcism network, and on that exact day, and time the exorcism takes place, anywhere from fifty to a hundred and fifty, maybe more, exorcists around the world in this network drop into deep meditative prayer to the Holy Spirit for a positive, and blessed outcome to the exact situation. I have witnessed this first hand, and the power this has as an ultimate weapon in these battles, well, there just aren't any words! Awe-inspiring and life-changing just doesn't do it!

I wake up every morning and pray that I never, ever, have to assist or take authority over an exorcism again. Not because I'm not prepared or scared, but because as rewarding as it can be to enjoy victory over these disgusting creatures, it is equally, and even more so, a horrific happening to witness, and be a part of and to realize what's at stake, can leave scars on you that never go away. Because I have gotten my preach on a little with the power of prayer, and because I'm so proud of the network I'm part of, and exorcism by distance, I will now share with you the possession case that I was called on to perform the rites.

I was not part of the assessment team, so there are some aspects of the situation I simply don't know about. The assessment team told me what they felt I needed to know to proceed. I will share that, and I will share how I took a slight outside the box approach, and how I relied on my discernment to bring closure to this case.

The location was an hour and a half drive outside of Las Vegas. My wife, Sharon, was still struggling with some health issues, and I really didn't want to expose whatever this was to her. So, I left her at home to heal up, and to take care of our two Mastiffs.

Another reason for heading out on my own on this one was because I had a terrible week leading up to getting the call to arms. Several bad day and night terrors, and a couple of times entering my home, receiving bad scratches on my right arm, twice while grabbing my front door knob to enter my home from outside. I couldn't help but wonder if this one was going to be the Motherload. Confession, Communion, and a lot of praying that week for sure.

Just before departing my home the morning of the event, I received a call from a minister there on site, who gave me a quick rundown on the small team that would be waiting there for me.

The team consisted of the minister, a woman who would be one of two prayer warriors. The other prayer warrior was a gentleman who was also going to be doing the filming. My two assistants were sisters, actual blood sisters. One a retired nurse, and the other a retired nun. The only other people in the home would be the client, a single mother (widowed), and the afflicted individual in question, her 18-year-old daughter.

Although I was an hour and a half or more away, and not even in my car yet, talking with this minister, and getting the rundown on what awaited me, it all of a sudden became very real… Although nothing was ever said to me, I honestly felt that my mentors and my friends throughout the network wanted to get as much of the homework, if you will, done for me so all I need to concentrate on was the task at hand, which was going to be the first exorcism I was to take authority over.

The minister had commented that, "All the grunt work had been done for me." I thought that was an amusing way to describe things.

He assured me that the young girl had been given a clean bill of health from her Doctor and that she had been seen by a Psychiatrist, and cleared to have no psychological issues. He added that there were a couple of strong prescription medications on board, but they were essential to her survival.

Most importantly, he wanted me to know that the powers that be throughout the association, the society, and the network, were overwhelmingly in agreement an exorcism was to be the next step. He explained that I was to sit down with the Mother when I got there, and have our own sit-down, and go over whatever I wanted with the Mother at that time.

I can't exactly tell you why, but at this moment just before leaving my home to get on the road, I felt the need to reach out to my extremely blessed, and gifted psychic/medium I knew and trusted that has a gift to remote view locations. It's not astral projection, and I'm not sure how it works, but she had helped me on many paranormal cases before, and I wanted to cover my bases and get her impressions on things...

I told her to take her time, and soon as she had something I needed to know, to call me, and I would pull over so we could talk, and that was it, I was off, and on the road.

The thing with living in the desert, is that everywhere you travel, you find yourself on these long desolate highways to what feels like nowhere, and you travel these long stretches of highway without seeing anything, another car, a house, town, nothing. It really gives you time to get into your own head, and try and figure things out.

I had only been on the road for about 45 minutes, and there it was, the call I was waiting for. It's always quite amazing when my friend does a remote viewing for me. This time she viewed a situation a little different than usual, and I wasn't sure what to expect to hear from her.

The first words out of her mouth were, "Rev, I'm sorry but if you had asked me to go, I would have to tell you I need to sit this one out." She went on to explain that she wasn't able to psychically stay there too long because it was too dangerous.

Whatever was taking place there was unlike any other location she had been to before for me. Her advice was, both hands on the wheel, don't speed, drive defensively, and be careful. Apparently, there were things, (and she didn't elaborate on what) that didn't want me to make it safely to my destination. I'm headed to a battleground, and there was something otherworldly there that owned the downstairs. There were three human spirits being held captive by this presence upstairs!

She said as soon as we hung up, she was headed to the nearest church to light a candle for me. I thanked her, I told her that I loved her as my sister in Christ, and said that may God be with you. I then continued on my journey...

I arrived at the client's home earlier than I thought I would. I must have been daydreaming. It's never a good sign when you pull up to a location, and the minister is waiting outside standing in the driveway.

This home had a cloak of darkness over it. The minister told me that he knew I was coming down the street, because "It started throwing objects around!" Of course, it's upset, the Lord is about to hand down the sentence.

Ideally, one would want this confrontation to take place on hallowed ground, so, time to step up my game, and think outside the box. I noticed there was a front yard water faucet with a garden hose connected. I always travel with a bag of blessed saint medals. I also save those small wires used to close the bags with bread in them. I grabbed a couple of medals, and connected them with a piece of wire to the faucet.

I laid hands on the faucet, and said some prayers of deliverance, and blessed the water system. I then began to spray down the roof with what was now Holy Water.

I asked the minister to open the front door for me and to hold it open until I entered the house. At the front door, I got down on my knees and began to pray out loud a special prayer I use before entering a home. Once I'm finished praying, I crawl on my hands and knees over the threshold of the home and enter. This is to show complete humility which is one of your greatest weapons against the demonic.

As I entered the home, I could hear quite a racket going on in the kitchen. All those gathered in the kitchen came walking out into the living room. I introduced myself and asked if someone was here doing some work in the kitchen.

One of them said, "No, all of the kitchen cabinet doors and drawers in the kitchen began to open, and close on their own, while you were praying!" I wanted to diffuse that right away, and commented, "Mere parlor tricks, nothing to be alarmed by!" I don't blame them, but they didn't seem to buy that one. It may not sound or seem very dramatic, but if you have ever been in a home where every bedroom closet, and bathroom door, and every drawer in every cabinet and dresser throughout the house are all opening and slamming shut by themselves all at once, and the sound is absolutely deafening, you simply cannot imagine how frightening that can be to witness!

And yes, we do refer to that as parlor tricks. That doesn't make it any less frightening.

I introduced myself to everyone, and they all gave me such a warm welcome. Then a young woman slowly approached me pushing a young girl in a wheelchair. I wasn't aware the girl in question was in a wheelchair.

The Mother introduced herself, and so did the daughter. The young girl grabbed hold of my hand and held on like she was never going to let go. She said something to me that I will never forget. She asked me if I was going to stay with her when he comes to take me?! I asked her when who comes to take you, she said the man my Father gave me to?!

I said, "Honey, no one's going to come, and take you anywhere."

She said, "Well, he's coming, he's coming soon." I told her that I needed to speak with her Mommy, and for her to stay with my friends. One of the sisters stepped forward, and grabbed hold of the wheelchair, and told the young girl that she needed to come talk with her while her Mother, and I visited for a bit, and wheeled her back into the kitchen.

The Mother and I sat on the couch, and the Mother said, " Oh my, where do I start?"

WOW, just WOW! This poor woman has spent the last 20 years sitting at the dinner table every night with the devil himself. She married a man that seemed normal enough at the time but soon realized that couldn't be further from the truth. It wasn't long after her marriage, she discovered her husband was a true witch, and Satanist. He had complete rule over his coven. The night her daughter was conceived, she said right at the exact moment of his climax, he looked up to the ceiling, and out loud declared his love for satan, and promised his seed, and child to satan.

She admitted that she couldn't wrap her mind around what he had just done, so she just laid there, and said nothing. They never had sex again after that night, and in a few weeks, she discovered that she was pregnant. Almost immediately after that, he became very abusive. He even told her once that he was only keeping her around until the baby was born. She honestly felt that her life and the baby's life were in danger. She plotted and executed a plan to run away.

She ran away all the way to the west coast from back east. It was a couple of years until he found out where she was. She never figured out how he found out. He even had a couple of his immediate blood relatives move out west to be close to her, and keep an eye on her for him. She did tell him once that she had bought a gun, and if she ever saw him again, she would kill him. She assumed he believed her because he never did come after her himself.

In the past 2 to 3 years, a slew of freak accidents have resulted in the deaths of her ex-husband, his sister, my client's sister, a man my client was dating for a few years, a close friend (a girlfriend), and a young girl who was a friend of her daughters!

At this time my client is just a little more than freaked out, and holding onto her sanity by her fingernails...

When her daughter was born, everything seemed normal at first. It wasn't too long before she noticed even as a baby, her daughter always acted as though she was seeing, and trying to communicate with others that Mom couldn't see. When the time came, and went when her daughter should be crawling, and then walking, but never did, she took her to a Doctor, and her daughter was diagnosed with a form of scoliosis. Her daughter eventually crawled, then managed to walk, with some difficulty, but she managed.

Her daughter went through the different levels of schooling, but never caught on, and her daughter hated school. It wasn't long after that she was diagnosed with ADHD. Not too long after that, her daughter began to have night, and day terrors all the time, and claimed she could also see ghosts.

As her daughter's afflictions intensified, she eventually became wheelchair bound and has been homeschooled for many years now. In the past couple of years, her daughter began to periodically have violent seizures and fits of violence. Her Mother described the seizures as though her daughter was fighting something off, and her violent fits as though she is someone or something else. She eventually sought out the help of the church, and now I'm here talking with her. She told me that more than one of my colleagues have commented that I'll save her daughter.

Nothing like a little extra added pressure, right? I told her I was ready to get started. She asked me if she could stay...

I said that absolutely she could, but she should go upstairs and pray, and no matter what she heard, don't come downstairs.

The Final Chapter
Exorcism by Distance
Part II

Preparation for the exorcism began with me making a couple of phone calls to important individuals to me who were going to send out urgent mass e-mails throughout the network, and alert all those available to participate, to begin prayer as soon as possible. I briefed everyone else on what their responsibilities were to be. I informed the two sisters who would be assisting me, that if I felt it necessary to do so, to prevent the demon from lashing out through the young girl, I would simply throw a blessed altar linen or chalice pall over the young girl's head. If need be, in addition to that I felt it would be sufficient restraint if they just put their hands on her shoulders to keep her sitting in her wheelchair. I asked the minister if he wouldn't mind staying in his car outside the home. If the neighbors heard anything inside the home to cause them to come by or call the authorities, he would be out there to greet them and try to discreetly explain what was going on.

I then asked the young girl if she was up for giving her confession to me. I told her it would just be her, and I, and we would just be in the kitchen. That way I could still have eyes on us, but be just far enough away, she and I could enjoy some privacy. I also told her after confession, I needed to baptize her. She agreed to both. The confession was pretty straight forward. My baptism consists of me putting the young girl's bare feet in a bowl of holy water, and then washing her feet with the holy water, as Christ did with the Apostles. It's also another way for me to show humility. It was now time to begin.

Instead of a stole, I choose to wear a religious relic rosary as a necklace.

I also have a second religious relic rosary that I have the afflicted wear as a necklace. I received as part of my discernment a secret phrase that only I know, and use. I whisper this phrase in the ear of the afflicted, and it is almost certain to bring the demon forward.

My discernment allows me to hear, and see demons when they are present. After they have manifested, I'm given more instructions psychically by divine intervention on what to say and look for guidance to give me any advantage. Sometimes I'm the only one who knows the unclean spirit is present. I ask all assisting me to just give the responses of the rites, and only do what I instruct them to do. No one is allowed to encourage or engage in dialogue with the entity.

This part is easier said than done, but I ask that they ignore anything the spirit is saying, especially if they are personally being addressed.

I whispered in the young girl's ear, and by the time I leaned back and straightened up, she was looking right at me with the glare of a predator! I witnessed the pupils of her eyes grow until they completely covered up the color of her eyes. The whites of the eyes slowly became bloodshot with some of the blood vessels appearing black. I'm hit in the chest with an arctic cold blast that engulfs me as if I just jumped into icy waters, followed by the smell of rotting meat. The smell of rotting meat is bad enough, but have you ever smelled rotting meat in a walk-in freezer?

Then in a voice that sounds like she has had a tracheotomy, the young (malevolent spirit) girl says to me, "Can you smell her rotting away?" followed by, "You're losing her just like Maggie!" Maggie was a former client who was possessed , and I lost her to a witch. The (unclean spirit) young girl comments, "I was looking forward to seeing Sharon again!" She (the young girl) doesn't know about Sharon as far as I knew.

As an exorcist, you have to have extremely thick skin, because the demon is not only going to throw everything that you love, and care about at you, it's also going to air all your dirty laundry in front of everyone there. If you're a closet alcoholic, struggling with a drug problem, had an affair, molested a child, struggling with sins of the flesh, addicted to porn, etc. you absolutely better be saved, and good with God.

I begin reciting the rites. Until the young girl is back with us, I'm going to refer to the demon as the unclean spirit. As the ritual continues, the unclean spirit takes turns looking at everyone in the room and attacking them verbally.

If that seems to be getting out of hand, without any warning, I will break from the rites, and blast the unclean spirit with Holy Water. I will occasionally change that up, and break from the rites, and kneel, and begin to pray the Hail Mary.

It's like hitting the demon in the head with a sledge hammer.

While I'm praying the Hail Mary, the unclean spirit begins to moan and groan, and cry out as though it's in excruciating agony, and pain. And I have no doubt that it is. Then I switch back up, and begin with the rites again, picking up right where I left off. It is interesting to watch the unclean spirit fidgeting around in the wheelchair, and look around into thin air, and address what I can only assume are other unclean spirits, trying to solicit help from them. Every once in a while the unclean spirit will look at something I can't see, and quickly lower its head or look away. I feel at those moments, it has seen an angelic presence there looking on at the situation. I guarantee you, there are representatives from both sides of the battle present!

    My main concern is for the young girl's health and well-being throughout this ordeal you absolutely cannot be concerned with time. It's as though time has stopped, and many people involved in performing, and assisting in the rites experience loss of time. We begin again. The young girl begins to laugh at me. I lean forward, and ask her, "Are you okay, what's so funny?" and I get spit on in my face, and she or the unclean spirit begins to laugh at me some more. We continue on. After a short period of time, I notice we have an audience. I notice an older gentleman, and two small girls standing on a landing halfway up the stairs watching the proceedings. I know these must be the ghosts my friend was talking about. I make eye to eye contact with each one of them. They had the oddest expressions on their faces. I'm not sure what emotions they were trying to convey to me. Then I'm startled by the unclean spirit shouting at me, "Fuck you, don't look at them, they're coming with me!" I blast it with holy water, look back, and the ghosts are gone. I look around at everyone, and so far, so good, everyone still seems to be okay.

I'm able to get through quite a bit of the rite without too much interruption other than one or two closet, and bedroom doors opening and slamming shut. I take a moment to gather my thoughts because I'm starting to feel easily distracted. I make the mistake of staring too long into the eyes of the unclean spirit, and the psychic attack begins.

I begin to clearly hear in my ears it's speaking to me, but the young girl's lips are not moving. It starts with threats. It goes down a list of everyone who is going to suffer because of my actions. My death on the way home is predicted, the return of Sharon's cancer, and then her death, and the one by one everyone there in the house is mentioned by name, and threatened. Even the souls of my parents and their parents aren't at rest, and will never be at rest as long as I'm on this current path I'm on. In an attempt to shut that down, I begin praying again. As

I'm praying I notice the young girl has positioned her feet, and legs in an unusual way, almost like cross-legged Indian style.

I get on my knees, and begin to grab a hold of her ankles, and gently pull her legs back down, and straighten them out. Just as I get her legs straight, and her feet almost onto the foot pedals, the wheelchair begins to move ever so slightly, rolling backward. I look up and notice the young girl's hands are in her lap, and my assistant standing behind her does not have her hands on the wheelchair at all. I grab ahold of the sides of the wheelchair and pull it forward to me. I then reach up and lock both back wheels. Then I notice the front wheels of the wheelchair begin to slightly raise up off the floor. I grab ahold of the front wheels and gently put them back on the floor. I continue to pray as I stand back up, and then continue on with the rites.

The unclean spirit has locked onto me with that predator stare, and the young girl's hands begin to ball up into fists, and she begins to slowly lean forward. I quickly grab the chalice pall and throw it over her face. She becomes dead still. What seems like minutes was probably just a few seconds, and she slowly leans back in the wheelchair, but her head doesn't stop, it flops all the way back over the back of the wheelchair with the sound of a thick branch snapping! We all jumped!! The way her head hung backward, and upside down, I can't speak for anyone else, but I thought she broke her neck.

The chalice pall never fell off her face, and she begins talking to my assistant behind me, I just had to do it, I pulled the chalice pall off her face so I could see if she was indeed speaking, and not just my imagination. I pull the chalice pall off, and you could hear the gasp in the room, especially from my assistant who was being spoken to. My assistant is standing there with one hand over her mouth. This was the sister who is the retired nun. The unclean spirit starts in on her with its head dangling there backward, and upside down. The unclean spirit brings up an incident that occurred when my assistant was still a nun, and out of respect for her, I'm not going to go into detail as to what was said, but my assistant and her sister were both clearly shaken. In an attempt to defuse this, I put one hand on the young girl, and start to pray out loud, (loud)! As I'm praying, the young girl begins to curl up in a ball in the wheelchair, and twist her torso around in an ungodly manner, and I did panic a little when I could see the deformity of her back, and head what sounded like marbles being crushed under a mill press. I quickly grab the altar linen and throw it completely over the young girl. Her head is still exposed, and the wheelchair spins around on its own, and now the young girl is facing me, and the unclean spirit has a few choice words for me. I ask for the two sisters to help me grab ahold of the young girl, and try to reposition her upright in the chair. As soon as we all grab ahold of her, she begins to have a demonic seizure. The difference between a demonic seizure and a grand mall is levitation. It is at this moment you do not let go of the afflicted, if you do a full on levitation occurs, excuse the expression, but all hell breaks loose...

The two sisters and I grab ahold of the young girl while she is clearly trying to come up out of the wheelchair. The wheelchair is actually bouncing up, and down in place. After a brief wrestling match, the young girl begins to vomit, urinate, and defecate all over herself. I know when this is over, we will be in the eye of the storm and have a calm period of time before the entity manifests for one last stand during this battle. When the seizure has passed, I instruct the two sisters with the help of the Mother, to take the young girl into the bathroom, and clean her up a bit. Besides the fact the wheelchair is a mess, I know I need to get the girl in a regular chair. I push the wheelchair out into the garage. At this point, I'm not going to be shocked by anything else, or so I thought until I ran right into the spirit of one of the ghost girls I saw upstairs earlier waiting for me in the garage. This ghost explained to me that it was her, her younger sister, and her grandfather remaining there attached to the property. They lived there first in their home. It caught fire and burned down, and the three of them died in the fire.

She said the entity I'm fighting came with the client's daughter. She added that they know they can go to heaven anytime, but when the malevolent entity arrived, it began tormenting them, and now won't let them leave. I told the ghost to stay upstairs with her family, and that angels would be coming soon to help them get to heaven. And, she was gone!

My discernment then started to really kick into overdrive. I'm being instructed to give the young girl communion. In my kit, I have both holy wine, and wafers that have been blessed, and turned into the body, and blood of Christ which I will use to complete this task.

Break time is over, everyone's ready, and you can feel the approaching storm, and we need to get ahead of it. I walk inside the house from the garage, and standing just inside the kitchen/garage door was one of the sisters waiting for me. She says, "Little one has a message for you, and wants to talk to you alone." I look over her shoulder and can see the young girl all cleaned up, and sitting at the kitchen table looking back at me. I muster the biggest smile for her that I can, and slowly walk over to her. I sit down next to her, and before she can say anything, I tell her she looks great, and ask her if she is okay. She begins by telling me how sorry she is for what happened, and that she's pretty embarrassed. I told her nonsense, that these things happen all the time, and not to be embarrassed because it is not her fault, followed by a big hug from me!

She then says to me that she has something to tell me, and it's not good. She says, "It also showed me your death!" She adds, "It also showed me where it's taking me when it comes back!"

I told her that everything it shows her, and everything it tells her are lies, and to not worry about anything.

She asks, "When are the angels coming?"

I said, "Very soon".

She says, "I hope so, because it's coming back, and it's not going to be alone." I took a moment to explain communion to her, and asked if she wanted to have Communion?

She started to cry and said, "Yes."

I gave her another hug, and told her to sit and relax for a moment while I had a quick pow-wow with the rest of the team. I find the whole team sitting on the stairs. They explain that the atmosphere in the living room has really changed, and thought it better if they waited on the stairs. I walk into the living room, and they were right. The living room seemed much darker, and colder. If there was another location in the house to go to, I would have. But, upstairs was off limits, and the kitchen was our safe zone. I instructed the team to get into position. I personally took the young girl into the living room and sat her down on a regular style high back chair.

We were so close to completing the rites during what I'm going to refer to as 'the first half of the exorcism' that I decide just to start over from the beginning. Before I continue on, I want to add that this team has gotten together a couple of times since this exorcism to compare notes so to speak and make sure we all saw, and experienced the same phenomena. And we did!

The second half of the exorcism was unique in the sense that something seemed to be laying in wait for us. Activity, paranormal, that is, came on so quickly, and things and events progressed so fast. It was very overwhelming, and I feel it caught us a bit off guard. I hadn't even begun yet, and my assistant behind the young girl says, "Let's see it move this chair," and God help us, at that very moment the chair, with the girl sitting it, spins around as if it was the wheelchair.

The girl is now staring at my assistant, and in the demon's voice says, "Hello sister." I reach out to grab the back of the chair and turn it around myself, and it suddenly spins back around, and now the young girl is looking right at me with the most unusual half smile I've ever seen. I glance up at my assistant who's looking right at me with a deer in the headlights stare.

I look back at her with the high eyebrow, and even though I didn't say anything, inside I was screaming, "DON'T PROVOKE!" The young girl's facial structure is actually different now. The eyes are almost black, just a little white showing. Now it smells as though we are all standing in a landfill!!

We continue on with the rites. The parlor tricks begin again. Front door bell begins to ring, and someone or something is knocking on the outside. It's not the minister, because the front door is not locked, and he could just walk in if he wanted to. I do my best to continue reciting the rites while observing phenomena too.

Shortly after that I notice the smoke from the burning Frankincense and Myrrh has drifted down to the floor and has become a mist on the entire floor. One of my assistants comments that her ears are all plugged up as if she is at a high altitude. We all agree that we all experiencing that very same feeling. A short time later, we all hear the automatic garage door open, and the client's car alarm, which was parked in the garage, go off. I instruct the prayer warrior to go upstairs, get the keys from the Mother, shut off the car alarm, and unplug the garage door opener.

We heard an odd thud at one of the windows in the living room. At this window was the ugliest mixed breed of dog, I think, appearing to be standing on its hind legs, with its paws on the outer window sill, and looking in the window at us, then it's gone.

We then hear what sounds like some kind of four-legged animal running around the living room. Everyone is looking around, down at the floor, and no one can see what's making this noise. Then it happened, my right-hand feels as though it just got caught in a bear trap! I'm still a little embarrassed that I screamed like a little girl, but I didn't break down. I did though, lose control of my right arm. It was numb, and just hanging there at my side, I couldn't move it.

The nurse, my assistant, who is behind me giving the responses asks, "What happened?"

I say, "Something bit my hand!"

We both look down, and my hand is swelling up bad, and quickly she says, "I have to get a pressure bandage on that." She asks, "Can you move your arm?"

I said, "No."

She says, "We have to get it in a sling." So, we had to take a quick unscheduled break. I grab both the altar linen, and the chalice pall, and cover the young girl's body with the linen, and put the pall over her head. The whole time I'm being attended to, the demon is just giggling under the pall.

Once I'm good to go, we resume. I pull the chalice pall off of the young girl's head, but I leave the altar linen on her body. She begins to squirm around under the linen. I cannot see what she's doing, but it doesn't sound good. Sounds like a large pepper grinder grinding walnuts with the shells on! I pull the linen off, and she has her feet and elbows on the chair where you sit. Her knees are up around her head now, and she has her head cocked up, looking at me.

The demon says to me, "Say goodbye, I'm taking her now!" This statement actually drops me to my knees, literally. Here I am, on my knees, and I'm just speaking to God as if he is right there. Speaking to Him from the heart.

As I'm praying, or talking to God, I should say, I begin to notice that a lot of light seems to be slowly making its way into the home. It comes down the stairway from upstairs. It seems to come from the garage door into the kitchen. Beams of light begin to come through the kitchen windows. The kitchen and that whole half of the house appear to be under direct sunlight, and an overwhelming smell of sweet bread baking comes over us.

There is a clear standoff between a force in the living room, and an even more powerful force in the kitchen, and upstairs about to completely take over. You can see the darkness in the living room slowly making its way back. I look up at the demon, and it is looking into the kitchen with a stare of amazement, and wonder. It is fixated on something and appears to be powerless.

I yell at it, "DEMON!" It looks right at me. I told it, I don't need to know your name, because God knows it! It then felt as though something else was speaking through me. I said, "You can't have this child, because she belongs to God. You are also being given a choice today. You were once deceived, and have spent your existence tormented, and tormenting. You can leap now into the abyss, and burn in the lava or you can crawl on your belly to the foot of the cross, and beg for forgiveness from God, His Son Jesus, His Mother Mary, and the Holy Spirit, and be allowed back into Heaven!" At that moment, the young girl's limbs relax and drop down. She sits up straight, and I can see in her face, it's her again. She has the most innocent look on her face. I asked her, "Are you ready to receive Communion?"

She nods yes. As I give her Communion, I quickly realize that there is no darkness in the house. It's as though we are standing outside. I look around, and everyone's crying tears of joy for sure! OK, are you sitting down? In the moments that followed, my right arm feels great. I pull it out of the sling and take the bandage off, and my arm looks as though nothing at all has happened to it. Nobody's talking, and you can hear someone crying, and praying. It's the client, the young girl's Mother, who is on her knees, sobbing, and praying. and STANDING OVER HER IS HER DAUGHTER! Not only standing but standing up straight with no hunchback.

Fast forward, it's been a while, but my client's daughter still has few minor health issues, but she is so happy, and enjoying a great life. The life God meant for her to have. The Mother has met and fallen in love with a wonderful man, they are planning to get married, and her daughter loves her new Stepfather.

After going through an ordeal like this team has just undergone, I always like to sit down with each one of them separately and have a one on one with them to make sure they are feeling alright. I like to know that they are processing emotionally everything that has happened in a healthy way. If they have anything that they really want to talk about, they have to get that off their chests.

If there are aspects of the events that have scared them, they have to address that, because things about what they experienced can infect your soul. I found it most interesting hearing everyone's take on being in the presence of The Holy Spirit! One assistant had an experience similar to mine; she smelled a most wonderful bakery aroma. One assistant was overcome by the strong overwhelming scent of the blessed incense. One assistant smelled wildflowers. The Mother upstairs heard music. She thought we had taken a break, and I was playing a CD of worship music. She also said that she saw angelic light beings on the top floor making their way downstairs. That matches what the young girl said.

Her daughter saw angelic light beings standing around me during Communion. The minister outside in his car felt a tremor. No one in the house felt the tremor. Something else that happened reminds me of an old, old saying that I think we can put to rest, "It's better to rule in hell, than serve in Heaven!"

RIGHT!

Many people who read this book will have their own theories about what really happened that day. Those of us in the know, know exactly what happened. As I finish this book, I will be on my knees sobbing, and praying that all my messages, here among these words find those truly in need, and allow them to hear what they are saying.

This book was a lifetime in the making, and my biggest regret was that I didn't write it sooner so that my parents could have read it. I know they were watching over me, and helping me write this book, so one day I will be able to sit with them, and start an afterlife book club with my autobiography first on the list to critique. I know this is going to sound silly to some, but as I finished writing my book, I was sitting in my kitchen area at the dining room table, and I had a direct view into the living room and could see the television. An oldie, but goodie movie was starting, and I took a break from writing to watch it again. The movie was "Field of Dreams." In addition to forgetting what an emotional sledgehammer to the head you get at the end, the movie also reminded me of how many years I wasted not coming out about my being able to see and hear spirit. I feel that there had to be many of them that I could have helped, but chose not to. If I knew then, what I know now, and had the chance to do it all over again, I wouldn't be so concerned with what people would think of me, and I would have shared my gift publicly. My Mother gave me that speech about seeing ghosts when I was ten, and even then, there were many times I even hid what I going through with my family. Remember, don't be me! If spirit is reaching out to you, YOU'RE NOT CRAZY, you're gifted!! And, this gift comes from a magical otherworld called, Heaven.

Try to create a little piece of Heaven around you every day, and share it with as many souls as you can.

Good Luck, and God Bless,
Rev. Shawn Whittington

PRAYERS

The Lord's Prayer

Our Father, Who art in heaven, hallowed be Thy name;
Thy kingdom come, Thy will be done on earth as it is in heaven.
Give us this day our daily bread, and forgive us our trespasses,
As we forgive those who trespass against us
And lead us not into temptation,
But deliver us from evil.
Amen.

The Hail Mary

Hail, Mary, full of Grace
The Lord is with thee;
Blessed art thou among women
And blessed is the fruit of thy womb, Jesus.
Holy Mary, Mother of God, pray for us sinners
Now and at the hour of our death.
Amen.

Prayer to St. Michael the Archangel

St. Michael the Archangel, defend us in the day of battle
Be our safeguard against the wiles and wickedness of the devil.
May God rebuke him, we humbly pray, and do thou, O prince
Of the heavenly host, by the power of God cast into hell Satan
And all the other evil spirits, who prowl through the world,
Seeking the ruin of souls.

Prayer of Authority

Lord Jesus Christ, in Thy Name,
I ask thee to bind and silence all powers and forces
that do not accept Thee as Lord and King,
In the air, in the water, in the ground,
The netherworld and nature and the spiritual world.
I ask Thee to bind all demonic action
And demonic communication.
Lord, seal this whole place, all of us here
And all our intentions in the Precious Blood
Of Jesus Christ.
Mary, we ask three to surround us

With thy mantle of protection
And crush Satan's power in our lives.
Saint Michael the Archangel, we ask you
And all our Guardian Angels
To defend us in battle against Satan
And the powers of darkness.
Amen.

<u>The Confiteor</u>

I confess to Almighty God,
To blessed Mary ever Virgin,
To blessed Michael the Archangel,
To blessed John the Baptist,
To the holy Apostles Peter and Paul,
And to all the saints,
That I have sinned exceedingly in thought,
Word and deed,
Through my fault, through my most grievous fault.
Therefore, I beseech blessed Mary ever Virgin,
Blessed Michael the Archangel,
Blessed John the Baptist,
The holy Apostles Peter and Paul,
And all the saints,
To pray to the Lord our God for me.

May Almighty God have mercy on me,
Forgive my sins,
And bring me to everlasting life. Amen.

May the almighty and merciful Lord
Grant me pardon, absolution,
And remission of all my sins. Amen.

The Litany of Humility

O Jesus, meek and humble of heart, hear me.
From the desire of being esteemed, deliver me, Jesus.
From the desire of being loved, deliver me, Jesus.
From the desire of being extolled, deliver me, Jesus.
From the desire of being honored, deliver me, Jesus.
From the desire of being praised, deliver me, Jesus.
From the desire of being preferred to others, deliver me, Jesus.
From the desire of being consulted, deliver me, Jesus.
From the desire of being approved, deliver me, Jesus.
From the fear of being humiliated, deliver me, Jesus.
From the fear of being despised, deliver me, Jesus.
From the fear of suffering rebukes, deliver me, Jesus.
From the fear of being calumniated, deliver me, Jesus.
From the fear of being forgotten, deliver me, Jesus.
From the fear of being ridiculed, deliver me, Jesus.
From the fear of being wronged, deliver me, Jesus.
From the fear of being suspected, deliver me, Jesus.
That others may be loved more than I, Jesus,
    Grant me the grace to desire it.
That others may be esteemed more than I, Jesus,
    Grant me the grace to desire it.
That in the opinion of the world, others may increase
And I may decrease, Jesus,
    Grant me the grace to desire it.

That others may be chosen and I set aside, Jesus,
>   Grant me the grace to desire it.
That others may be praised and I unnoticed, Jesus,
>   Grant me the grace to desire it.
That others may be preferred to me in everything, Jesus,
>   Grant me the grace to desire it.
That others may become holier than I, provided that I
Become as holy as I should, Jesus,
>   Grant me the grace to desire it.

House Blessing

All the items listed below need to be purchased, then taken to a priest (to be blessed).
>   Frankincense incense plus incense burner
>   Distilled water for holy water.
>   Kosher and sea salt.
>   Extra virgin olive oil.
>   White chalk.

Burn the frankincense, and smoke out the home well, every room, closets, bathrooms, and garage. Basement and attic if the home has these spaces.

Sprinkle the holy water in every room on every wall in the sign of the cross. Put your finger in the holy water, and physically touch the wall, and make the sign of the cross. Do this also with the holy oil, and blessed chalk.

Sprinkle the blessed salts on every window sill, and on the floor at the base of every door, that leads outside.

Above the front door on the outside, draw three crosses, and the date.

For you Christian and Catholics, stand in the most center part of the house, and recite the prayer of authority.

For the spiritual, say out loud that you command any, and all malevolent, unclean or demonic entities to leave your home. You rebuke their presence, and they are not welcome, and must leave immediately.

Even on what should be a routine house blessing, if you suspect the demonic may be present, there are two things you can do to prevent the situation from escalating to a dangerous level.

Demons do not want to be detected. For daytime blessings, have some blessed baby powder on hand. If you feel a demonic entity is hiding in a corner or standing right next to you, put a small amount of blessed powder in your hand, raise your palm up, and blow the powder into the air into the direction you feel the oppressiveness. For some reason only known to God, the blessed powder sticks to the entity, and once they realize you can see them, they will flee for the time being.

For nighttime blessings, have a large blessed white candle and a large crucifix. If you suspect someone in the household is under demonic oppression, hold the crucifix in front of the person's face, hold the candle up to the cross, and cast the shadow of the cross onto the person's face. Demons cannot stand being in the shadow of the cross, and will un-attach itself from the victim, long enough for you to get the person engaged in prayer. Both techniques are temporary, and just buy you enough time to complete the house blessing.

PHOTO GALLERY

Lawrence William Whittington and Edith Morace Whittington

Lawrence William Whittington

Orbs don't have that WOW Factor but, need to be in the conversation. This selfie caught this Orb form sneaking up behind me. I turned around and came face to face with a woman (Ghost), staring at me. She did not move until I stepped out of her way!

Witnessed this orb come out of a master bedroom, float down a hallway and across the living room, hover for a moment over flowers that I brought and then up the chimney it went. Don't hold it against the ghost if all it can do is appear as an orb.

God, Ghosts And The Paranormal Ministry

Apparition caught in a deserted desert cemetery

Apparition of a cowboy (Ghost) in an old saloon.

Demon eyes staring at me through a window just before my severe demonic attack

Sharon can't see the spirit that is communicating with her here but, its reflection showed up in the window in the background

Ghost of female matriarch caught in reflection of mirrored pillar in haunted mansion during investigation

Photo bombed by the spirit attached to this home during property blessing

Demonic apparition (No head, hands or feet), caught at top of stairs

Demonic black mass at top of stairs under landing

Hand of a ghost in a haunted library looking for some good reading material

Demonic entity posing as a child following me

God, Ghosts And The Paranormal Ministry

A friend (ghost), at a Southern Nevada ghost town

The ghost of Bonnie or Clyde (not sure which), hanging around their death car

"The Rev" and his lovely wife Sharon

About The Author

Deliverance Minister/Radio Host/Author

Reverend Shawn P. Whittington is an ordained Exorcism/Deliverance Minister, ghostbuster, lecturer and teacher of paranormal studies at a Bible College and Theological Seminary. Shawn, and his wife, Sharon, (who is an ordained Lutheran minister and intuitive) are both survivors of extreme demonic attacks and together have over 40 years of in the field experience. They founded and operate Ghost-B-Gone which is a Spiritual Warfare service based in Las Vegas, Nevada assisting with paranormal problems of various types and severity.

Since 2015, Shawn is the host of Vegas Supernatural Radio show which can be heard Mondays at 8pm EST on KCOR Radio (Kcorradio.com)

GOD, GHOSTS, AND THE PARANORMAL MINISTRY: A Supernatural and Spiritual Autobiography by Rev. Shawn P. Whittington (Stellium Books March 17, 2019) is a raw and truthful account of his experiences.

For more information:
Ghost B Gone website
https://www.ghost-b-gone.biz/
Contact: Phone: 702.416.6288
Email: Shawn@ghost-b-gone.biz